So you <u>really</u> want to learn
Junior Maths
Book 1

GALORE PARK

So you really want to learn

Junior Maths

Book 1

David Hillard

Series Editor: Louise Martine

www.galorepark.co.uk

Published by Galore Park Publishing Ltd
19/21 Sayers Lane, Tenterden, Kent TN30 6BW

www.galorepark.co.uk

Layout by Typetechnique
Technical illustrations by Graham Edwards
Cartoon illustrations by Gwyneth Williamson
Cover design by The Design Gallery

Printed by Replika Press Pvt Ltd, India

ISBN: 978 1 905735 21 1

First published 2008, reprinted 2008, 2009, 2011

To accompany this course:
Junior Maths Book 1 Answer Book   ISBN: 978 1 905735 22 8
Junior Maths Book 1 Worksheets   D0122001

Junior Maths Book 1 Worksheets are available as a chargeable download using the
above code. Full details can be found at www.galorepark.co.uk

Details of other Galore Park publications are available at www.galorepark.co.uk

ISEB Revision Guides, publications and examination papers may also be obtained
from Galore Park.

The publishers are grateful for permission to use the photographs as follows:
Chapter 8: page 100 David N. Davis/Science Photo Library (L); Mark Newman/Science
Photo Library (C); Peter Chadwick/Science Photo Library (R); Chapter 9: page 101
Helene Rogers/Alamy (L); Helene Rogers/Alamy (R); Chapter 12: page 149 A. Crump,
Tdr, Who/Science Photo Library (R); Chapter 13: page 154 Martyn F. Chillmaid/Science
Photo Library (L); page 154 Martyn F. Chillmaid/Science Photo Library (L); page 154
Gavin Kingcome/Science Photo Library (C); Chapter 14: page 161 Lew Merrim/Science
Photo Library.

About the author

David Hillard has spent more than 45 years teaching mathematics in two preparatory schools. Generally he has taught those who would not describe themselves as particularly proficient at the subject.

Since 1980 he has been associated with the Common Entrance Examination at 11+, 12+ and 13+ levels in the role of either adviser, assessor or setter. He played a significant part in the revision of the syllabus in 2003 when the present format of the examination was introduced.

He is a co-author of the successful *Fundamental Mathematics* series, first published in 1984.

Preface

The teaching of mathematics never ceases to cause intense discussion. Modern methods have mystified both parents and children alike. Even the DfES has expressed a wish to return to the '*standard method*'. At present great emphasis is laid on a '*mental*' approach with formality of method introduced later. Mental ability and agility are important and would be omitted at a loss. There must, however, be room for both approaches without being prescriptive.

In the final analysis it is the interests of the child that are paramount. For those who are mathematically adept the '*mental*' approach will be both challenging and rewarding. There are others, however, who will find this method difficult and beyond their comprehension. This will often produce a sense of frustration and a negative attitude which can lead to the 'I can't do maths' syndrome. Children want to succeed so that they gain in confidence and self esteem. Sometimes they need to be told what to do.

The intention of this book is to provide Year 3 with enough material to appeal to all abilities and satisfy all needs. It is not laid out in any teaching order but rather by topic. The author envisages a chapter being revisited during the course of the year.

Mental strategy is best gained by general discussion. There is often more than one approach to be considered. Chapter 25: Mental strategies covers far more ground than can be covered in a year and must be used as and when the child is ready.

The author has never believed in telling teachers what they should or should not do. It is entirely up to them to produce the correct material at the appropriate time: they know what the child requires – every one is different. Hopefully all will be stimulated but, more importantly, they should enjoy the subject. Have fun and I hope you don't run out of material!

Acknowledgements

Acknowledgements is another word for saying thank you to the very many people who, together, make up a production team. Firstly my thanks to Galore Park, and in particular to Louise Martine, for believing that I could produce what they wanted and to Teresa Sibree who helped enhance the original manuscript. I am grateful for the encouragement given by my ex-colleagues at Wellesley House, in particular Carolyn who helped test much of the material, and also my thanks to Pauline, Jonathan and Michael for their invaluable technical assistance. There is a host of others who should be mentioned; they know who they are and I am grateful to all of them.

David Hillard
February 2008

Contents

Chapter 1: Place value

We are going to start our exciting journey through the wonders of mathematics by making sure that we understand the basics of how numbers are formed. As you know, we have ten symbols (known as figures or digits) that we use to make up all our numbers:

0	1	2	3	4	5	6	7	8	9
zero	one	two	three	four	five	six	seven	eight	nine

When these numbers stand alone they mean what they say:

4 girls   *7 boys*

But what happens when we want to count above nine? We have to use more than one digit to create a new number. But when we put two or more digits together, they start to mean different things.

Units, tens and hundreds

What each digit means depends on the position (or place) of the digit in the number. This is called the **place value** of the digit. Let's look at the number twenty-two.

Twenty-two is written as **22**

Both digits are the same – but they don't mean the same!

Let's put this number in columns to help you understand what each digit means:

Tens	Units
T	U
2	2

Remember that a 2 in the **Units** column means the number has 2 units.

Remember that a 2 in the **Tens** column means the number has 2 tens. 2 tens is 20.

Here's another example:

Five hundred and fifty-five is written as **555**

All three digits are the same but, again, they mean different things.

Hundreds	Tens	Units
H	T	U
5	5	5

The 5 in the **Units** column means the number has 5 units.

The 5 in the **Tens** column means the number has 5 tens. 5 tens is 50

The 5 in the **Hundreds** column means the number has 5 hundreds. 5 hundreds is 500

Summary

Thousand	Hundred	Ten	Unit
1000	100	10	1

Each column is 10 times larger than its right-hand neighbour.

One thousand is 10 times larger than one hundred. We will meet thousands again as we go through the book.

Exercise 1.1: Making numbers

Your teacher will ask you to take some number cards. Each card has a single digit written on it.

1. You are going to use different combinations of cards to make some numbers. Each time, make and record:

   (i) the smallest number; (ii) the largest number; (iii) all possible numbers.

   (a) First, use two number cards to make your numbers. Make sure the cards are different. Do not choose a 0

   (b) Now make numbers using three cards. Again, make sure the cards are all different and do not choose a 0

   (c) This time, use two number cards, but make sure one of them is 0

   Remember that 0 has no value on its own.

   (d) Finally, use three number cards. Make sure that one of them is 0 and that the other two are different.

2. What difference does having a 0 make to the numbers you can create?

3. See what happens if the numbers are not all different.

Writing numbers in words and digits

We have to think about place value when we write a number down, whether in words or in numbers.

Examples:

(i) Write the number 526 in words.
Five hundred and twenty-six.

(ii) Write the number four hundred and six in figures.
The first part of the number is 'four hundred',
so we know that it has three digits, and the first is 4

There are no 'tens' in the number, so the next digit is 0

There are 6 units

So four hundred and six in figures is 406

H	T	U
4	?	?
4	0	?
4	0	6

Exercise 1.2: Writing numbers

1. Write these numbers in words:

   (a) 47   (d) 119   (g) 207   (j) 999

   (b) 60   (e) 191   (h) 589

   (c) 83   (f) 270   (i) 628

2. Write these numbers in figures:

   (a) Fourteen   (f) Three hundred and six

   (b) Thirty-six   (g) Four hundred and fifty-three

   (c) Ninety-five   (h) Six hundred and forty-eight

   (d) Two hundred and fifteen   (i) Seven hundred and forty

   (e) Two hundred and fifty-one   (j) Nine hundred and nine

3. Write down the real value of the underlined digit:

   (a) 4$\underline{3}$ (d) 6$\underline{6}$ (g) $\underline{6}$0   (j) 40$\underline{7}$

   (b) $\underline{4}$29   (e) $\underline{6}$66   (h) 3$\underline{1}$0

   (c) 6$\underline{6}$6   (f) 1$\underline{6}$4   (i) $\underline{2}$00

4. Write down the real value of the underlined digit:

   (a) 7$\underline{4}$5   (f) $\underline{8}$047

   (b) $\underline{9}$27   (g) 3$\underline{1}$60

   (c) 83$\underline{9}$ (h) $\underline{9}$099

   (d) $\underline{1}$843   (i) 483$\underline{0}$

   (e) 56$\underline{1}$9   (j) 5$\underline{0}$42

Ordering numbers

When you are asked to put numbers in order these are some of the words you may come across: smallest, largest, highest, lowest, longest, shortest, heaviest and lightest.

The more digits a number has the larger it is.

Example: 102 is larger than 98

If there are the same number of digits, **place value** decides the size of the number.

Examples:

(i) 37 and 51
     51 is larger because 5 tens (50) is larger than 3 tens (30).

(ii) 37 and 22
     37 is larger because 3 tens (30) is larger than 2 tens (20).

If the first left-hand digits are the same, we need to look at the next digit.

Examples:

(i) 746 and 763

     Both numbers start with 700, so **look at the next digit to the right**.

     60 is larger than 40
     So 763 is larger than 746

(ii) 574 and 578

     The first two digits are the same, so **look at the last right-hand digit**.

     8 is larger than 4
     So 578 is larger than 574

Done
13/02/12

Exercise 1.3: Ordering numbers

1. Write these numbers in order of size, starting with the **largest**:

    (a) 74   28
    (b) 69   96
    (c) 47   46
    (d) 143   286
    (e) 419   398
    (f) 316   304
    (g) 429   430
    (h) 738   735
    (i) 817   871
    (j) 410   401

    (k) 87   9   78
    (l) 11   101   10
    (m) 326   623   236
    (n) 300   298   303
    (o) 204   402   240
    (p) 524   245   452   425
    (q) 147   741   471   417
    (r) 143   341   431   314   413
    (s) 456   645   546   654   465
    (t) 579   975   759   795   597   957

2. Write these numbers in order of size, starting with the **smallest**:

    (a) 27   36
    (b) 73   37
    (c) 218   527
    (d) 386   123
    (e) 496   512
    (f) 986   860
    (g) 410   401
    (h) 223   233
    (i) 716   761
    (j) 167   617

    (k) 87   110   101
    (l) 232   7   30
    (m) 67   59   72
    (n) 300   33   30
    (o) 342   633   463
    (p) 717   747   727   707
    (q) 229   224   227   220
    (r) 103   301   131   311   113
    (s) 437   473   734   243   234
    (t) 523   325   253   235   532   352

Exercise 1.4: Summary exercise

1. Using the digits 7, 9 and 3, write down:

    (a) the largest number you can;

    (b) the smallest number you can.

2. Using the digits 2, 5 and 4, write down:

    (a) as many different two-digit numbers as you can;

    (b) as many different three-digit numbers as you can.

3. Write:

    (a) the number 717 in words;

    (b) four hundred and two in figures.

4. Write down the real value of the underlined digit:

    (a) 3<u>7</u>4   (b) 18<u>6</u>   (c) <u>4</u>19   (d) <u>3</u>683

5. Write these numbers in order of size, starting with the **largest**:

    (a) 64   46   66

    (b) 76   87   67   78

    (c) 357   735   537   573   375   753

6. Write these numbers in order of size, starting with the **smallest**:

    (a) 21   12   15

    (b) 221   230   203   212

    (c) 123   321   231   213   132   312

End of chapter activity: Understanding place value

This classroom game can help you to understand place value. It is fun to play and all you need is a couple of dice.

Divide the class into two teams and give each team a die. The teacher can put the names of the two teams on the white board. The aim of the game is for each team to create a number by rolling the die. The teacher will set a challenge, for example, she may say: 'who can create the largest two-digit number?'

She would write on the board:

Team A		Team B	
Tens	**Units**	**Tens**	**Units**
–	–	–	–

Team A would roll their die. They must decide where to place the number shown so that they have the best chance of winning by creating the largest number. Should it go in the units or the tens column? Say, for example, they threw a six, it would make most sense to put it in the tens column so it becomes 6 tens. If a 2 was rolled it would make sense perhaps to put it in the units column because there is a good chance that they could throw a higher number next time which they could put in the tens column and so improve their chance of winning.

Team B would then throw their die and decide whether to put their number in the tens or units column.

Team A would throw again and the number put in the remaining position. Team B would then do the same.

The winning team would be the team that has created the highest number.

This game can be extended to creating three and four-digit numbers. The challenge might be to make the highest number or indeed the lowest number possible from the numbers generated by the roll of a die.

Did you know?

'Googol' is the mathematical term for a **1 followed by a hundred zeros**!

10 000 000 000 000 000 000 000 000 000 000 000 000 000 000 000 000 000 000 000 000 000 000 000 000 000 000 000 000 000 000 000 000 000 000

The number googol was the inspiration for the name of the internet search engine Google.

Chapter 2: Counting

Counting is the first mathematical thing everyone does. You probably remember using your fingers to help you! The quicker you are able to count, and the more agile you are with numbers, the easier you will find it to work out your answers.

The following exercises will help you count in your head more quickly, which will help when you do mental work. They should be used only when your teacher thinks you are ready for them. You can answer either orally or on paper. (All your answers should be more than 0 and less than 1000)

Exercise 2.1: Counting in units

1. Count on in ones starting from:

    (a) 3   (b) 17   (c) 40   (d) 93

2. Count back in ones starting from:

    (a) 6   (b) 19   (c) 50   (d) 109

Exercise 2.2: Counting in twos

1. Count on in twos starting from:

    (a) 2   (b) 3   (c) 28   (d) 87

2. Count back in twos starting from:

    (a) 12   (b) 25   (c) 40   (d) 103

Exercise 2.3: Counting in threes

1. Count on in threes starting from:

    (a) 3   (b) 11   (c) 48   (d) 99

2. Count back in threes starting from:

    (a) 7   (b) 18   (c) 53   (d) 104

Exercise 2.4: Counting in fours

1. Count on in fours starting from:

   (a) 4   (b) 15   (c) 50   (d) 81

2. Count back in fours starting from:

   (a) 11   (b) 49   (c) 74   (d) 112

Exercise 2.5: Counting in fives

1. Count on in fives starting from:

   (a) 5   (b) 43   (c) 51   (d) 94

2. Count back in fives starting from:

   (a) 21   (b) 53   (c) 72   (d) 104

Exercise 2.6: Counting in tens

1. Count on in tens starting from:

   (a) 10   (b) 67   (c) 154   (d) 496

2. Count back in tens starting from:

   (a) 70   (b) 210   (c) 353   (d) 484

Exercise 2.7: Counting in multiples of ten

1. Count on in 20s starting from:

   (a) 20   (b) 55   (c) 147   (d) 296

2. Count on in 30s starting from:

   (a) 30   (b) 80   (c) 134   (d) 298

3. Count back in 40s starting from:

   (a) 90   (b) 110   (c) 278   (d) 404

4. Count on in 50s starting from:

    (a) 50   (b) 80   (c) 215   (d) 435

5. Count back in 50s starting from:

    (a) 190   (b) 210   (c) 450   (d) 775

Exercise 2.8: Counting in multiples of one hundred

1. Count on in 100s starting from:

    (a) 100   (b) 70   (c) 143   (d) 249

2. Count back in 100s starting from:

    (a) 1000   (b) 650   (c) 525   (d) 481

3. Count on in 200s starting from:

    (a) 100   (b) 400   (c) 5   (d) 537

4. Count back 3 100s starting from:

    (a) 500   (b) 1000   (c) 301   (d) 743

· ·

Nines

Adding nine

The number 9 is interesting to work with. You can think of it as (10 − 1). So if you want to add 9 to a number, simply add 10 first and then subtract 1

Example:	14 + 9
	Think of this as:
	14 + 9 = 14 + 10 − 1
	= 24 − 1
	= 23

Exercise 2.9: Counting on in nines

1. Work out:

   (a) 10 + 9   (f) 67 + 9

   (b) 4 + 9   (g) 91 + 9

   (c) 8 + 9   (h) 79 + 9

   (d) 12 + 9   (i) 43 + 9

   (e) 35 + 9   (j) 96 + 9

2. Count on in 9s:

   (a) from 9 until you reach 63

   (b) from 13 until you reach 103

3. Calculate:

   (a) 300 + 9   (f) 846 + 9

   (b) 247 + 9   (g) 914 + 9

   (c) 401 + 9   (h) 525 + 9

   (d) 668 + 9   (i) 809 + 9

   (e) 790 + 9   (j) 289 + 9

· Chapter 2 · · · ·

Subtracting nine

To subtract 9 from a number, simply subtract
10 first and then add 1

Example:	$17 - 9 = 17 - 10 + 1$
	$= 7 + 1$
	$= 8$

Exercise 2.10: Counting back in nines

1   Calculate:

(a) 12 − 9   (f) 23 − 9

(b) 19 − 9   (g) 45 − 9

(c) 16 − 9   (h) 87 − 9

(d) 70 − 9   (i) 54 − 9

(e) 38 − 9   (j) 91 − 9

2.   Calculate:

(a) 430 − 9   (f) 655 − 9

(b) 219 − 9   (g) 813 − 9

(c) 475 − 9   (h) 462 − 9

(d) 392 − 9   (i) 184 − 9

(e) 709 − 9   (j) 996 − 9

3.   Count back in 9s:

(a) from 108 until you reach 63

(b) from 75 until you reach 3

. . . .

Elevens

Adding eleven

There is a neat little trick we can play with eleven too. It is so much easier if you think of 11 as (10 + 1).

To add 11 to a number, simply add 10 first and then add 1

Example:	$17 + 11 = 17 + 10 + 1$
	$= 27 + 1$
	$= 28$

Exercise 2.11: Counting on in elevens

1. Calculate:

   (a) 5 + 11
   (b) 9 + 11
   (c) 14 + 11
   (d) 31 + 11
   (e) 49 + 11

   (f) 28 + 11
   (g) 87 + 11
   (h) 60 + 11
   (i) 36 + 11
   (j) 93 + 11

2. Calculate:

   (a) 426 + 11
   (b) 148 + 11
   (c) 780 + 11
   (d) 467 + 11
   (e) 274 + 11

   (f) 102 + 11
   (g) 945 + 11
   (h) 161 + 11
   (i) 673 + 11
   (j) 389 + 11

3. Count on in 11s:

   (a) from 11 until you reach 77

   (b) from 27 until you reach 104

· ·

Subtracting eleven

To subtract 11, simply subtract 10 first and then subtract another 1

Example:	35 − 11 = 35 − 10 − 1
	= 25 − 1
	= 24

Exercise 2.12: Counting back in elevens

1. Calculate:

    (a) 14 − 11   (f) 80 − 11

    (b) 19 − 11   (g) 97 − 11

    (c) 31 − 11   (h) 72 − 11

    (d) 46 − 11   (i) 65 − 11

    (e) 58 − 11   (j) 23 − 11

2. Calculate:

    (a) 143 − 11   (f) 638 − 11

    (b) 273 − 11   (g) 739 − 11

    (c) 322 − 11   (h) 990 − 11

    (d) 446 − 11   (i) 571 − 11

    (e) 240 − 11   (j) 147 − 11

3. Count back in 11s:

    (a) from 132 until you reach 77

    (b) from 151 until you reach 52

Exercise 2.13: Summary exercise

1. Write down the number that is 10 more than:

    (a) 8   (c) 93   (e) 591

    (b) 27   (d) 445

2. Write down how many 10s have been added to make:

    (a) 40 into 90   (c) 23 into 93   (e) 678 into 738

    (b) 560 into 620   (d) 227 into 277

3. How much larger is:

   (a) 80 than 10   (c) 235 than 205   (e) 749 than 679

   (b) 110 than 90   (d) 497 than 457

4. What number is 10 less than:

   (a) 13   (c) 286   (e) 704

   (b) 68   (d) 300

5. How many 10s have been subtracted to make:

   (a) 70 become 40   (c) 76 become 16   (e) 541 become 481

   (b) 430 become 370 (d) 287 become 217

6. How much smaller is:

   (a) 30 than 80   (c) 126 than 186   (e) 384 than 454

   (b) 270 than 320   (d) 286 than 306

7. What number is 100 more than:

   (a) 63   (b) 325

8. How many 100s have been added to make:

   (a) 14 become 414   (b) 273 become 973

9. How much smaller is:

   (a) 270 than 870   (b) 56 than 456

10. What number is 100 less than:

   (a) 840   (b) 123

11. How many 100s have been added to make:

   (a) 20 become 520   (b) 637 become 937

12. How much larger is:

   (a) 206 than 6   (b) 871 than 271

End of chapter activity: Lumbers!

Lumbers are numbers represented by letters as follows:

1	2	3	4	5	6	7	8	9	0
a	b	c	d	e	f	g	h	i	j

So   ae is 15

      ejc is 503

      dh + i = 48 + 9 = 57

      ej − aa = 50 − 11 = 39

Calculate the following, giving your answers as numbers:

1. ic + aj   163
2. ch + bj
3. hg + cj
4. dj + bd
5. ih + ej
6. bgc + ajj
7. bjg − aj
8. age − bj
9. aaj − cj
10. bci − dj
11. ajf − ajj
12. eee − ejj

13. hi + i
14. i + adb
15. i + big
16. hc − i
17. ajg − i
18. cjj − i
19. aa + bi
20. adj + aa
21. ig + aa
22. ag − aa
23. bhj − aa
24. cjg − aa

Did you know?

The Aztecs used signs or symbols to show numbers.

The number one was shown by a dot: ●

They counted in 20s. A flag stood for 20

A feather-like sign stood for 400

and 8000 was shown by a pouch for carrying incense

Chapter 3: Addition

We have already come across addition in Chapter 2 – in this chapter we are going to look at it in more detail. There is also a lot about addition and how we can do it in our heads in Chapter 25: Mental strategies.

Let us start with two simple questions:

> What is the answer to 3 + 1?

> What is the answer to 1 + 3?

Was the answer 4 in each case? Yes. This shows us that it does not matter in which order numbers are **added** – the answer will be the same.

· ·

Exercise 3.1: Addition square

1. Copy and complete this addition square

+	1	2	3	4	5	6	7	8	9	10
1	2	3								
2	3									
3										
4				9				13		
5			9							
6										
7										
8										
9			13							
10										20

These are called **number bonds**. You should learn these thoroughly. Remember that you need learn only half of them because you know that:

6 + 4 = 10   and   4 + 6 = 10

Pairs that add up to ten

You should look for pairs of numbers that add up to 10

$1 + 9 = 10$ $9 + 1 = 10$

$2 + 8 = 10$ $8 + 2 = 10$

$3 + 7 = 10$ $7 + 3 = 10$

$4 + 6 = 10$ $6 + 4 = 10$

$5 + 5 = 10$

You can use these pairs to help you when you have several numbers to add together.

Tip: Use your number bonds to ten to find the pairs of numbers to add together first.

Examples:

(i) $7 + 3 + 4 = 10 + 4$

$= 14$

(ii) $5 + 9 + 1 = 5 + 10$

$= 15$

(iii) $4 + 7 + 6 = 10 + 7$

$= 17$

Exercise 3.2: Simple addition

1. Try to find a 10 when adding these numbers together. Set out your work as shown in the examples above:

(a) 2 + 8 + 3

(b) 4 + 3 + 7

(c) 5 + 2 + 5

(d) 4 + 9 + 1

(e) 4 + 7 + 3

(f) 6 + 4 + 1 + 5

(g) 1 + 5 + 3 + 7

(h) 2 + 3 + 8 + 1

(i) 1 + 5 + 2 + 9

(j) 8 + 5 + 1 + 5

(k) 3 + 4 + 6 + 6

(l) 7 + 4 + 2 + 3

(m) 1 + 4 + 6 + 9

(n) 6 + 1 + 9 + 4

(o) 5 + 4 + 2 + 4

2. Calculate the answers to the following questions in your head.

Tips: It often helps if you put the largest number first. Remember that the words **plus** and **sum** mean **add** in mathematics.

(a) 6 + 4

(b) 5 + 8

(c) 7 + 6

(d) 5 + 9

(e) 8 + 8

(f) What is the total of 8 + 3?

(g) Find the sum of 4 and 9

(h) 7 plus 4

(i) Add 10 and 8

(j) Increase 5 by 6

(k) 3 + 2 + 1

(l) 2 + 4 + 6

(m) 3 + 5 + 7

(n) 8 + 5 + 2

(o) 10 + 4 + 5

(p) 8 + 7 + 5

(q) 6 + 5 + 4 + 3

(r) 2 + 4 + 6 + 8

(s) 4 + 3 + 3 + 4

(t) 2 + 3 + 5 + 7

The formal method of addition

There is another way of setting out your work, one which will be very familiar to your parents. Let's look at how we do it by starting with the very simple calculation we saw at the beginning of this chapter: 3 + 1

Example: 3 + 1

Step 1:   First of all, set out the digits in their correct columns.

Remember: units under **Units** column.

3 + 1 is set out as

	U
	3
+	1

Step 2:   Add the units in the **Units** column together and put the answer under the numbers, below the line.

	U
	3
+	1
	4

And there you have your answer, 4!

Now let's look at a calculation that is made up of numbers with two digits.

Example: 64 + 23

Step 1:   Start by setting out the digits in their correct columns.

This time we have **units** and **tens**. Remember: units under **Units** column, tens under **Tens** column.

So, 64 + 23 is set out as

	T	U
	6	4
+	2	3

Step 2:	Add the **Units** column.

Put your answer under the digits in the **Units** column, below the line.

	T	U
	6	4
+	2	3
		7

Step 3:	Now move over to the next column, the **Tens** column, and add together the tens digits.

Put your answer under the digits in the **Tens** column, below the line.

	T	U
	6	4
+	2	3
	8	7

Use Exercise 3.3 to practise doing this yourself.

Exercise 3.3: Formal addition

1.
	T	U
	3	0
+	1	1

2.
	T	U
	3	6
+	3	2

3.
	T	U
	2	1
+	2	4

4. 32 + 44

5. 62 + 15

6. 21 + 32

7. 17 + 72

8. 45 + 43

9. 18 + 51

10. 46 + 23

11. 17 + 21

12. 24 + 61

13. 53 + 23

14. 73 + 16

15. 16 + 51

16. 43 + 52

17. 32 + 12

18. 42 + 44

19. 17 + 82

20. 76 + 13

These were easy because the digits in each column added up to a number less than 10. But what happens if the two digits add up to 10 or more. Let's look at a couple of examples using two different methods.

> **Tip:** Remember what we learnt about **place value** in Chapter 1. For example, thirteen is written as 13, which means 1 ten and 3 units.

Method 1

Example: 24 + 38

Step 1: First set out the digits in their correct columns.

Step 2: Then add the digits in the **Units** column.

	T	U
	2	4
+	3	8
	1	2

4 + 8 = 12 which is 1 ten and 2 units. Put the 1 in the **Tens** column and the 2 in the **Units** column.

Step 3: Now add the digits in the **Tens** column.

	T	U
	2	4
+	3	8
	1	2
	5	0

When adding the digits in the **Tens** column, remember that you are adding 2 tens and 3 tens
20 + 30 = 50
Write down the answer 50 by putting the 5 in the **Tens** column and the 0 in the **Units** column.

Step 4: Finally add the two answers 12 + 50 together.

	T	U
	2	4
+	3	8
	1	2
	5	0
	6	2

Add 12 + 50 to give the answer 62

Method 2

Example: 48 + 35

Step 1:   First set out the digits in their correct columns.

Step 2:   Then add the digits in the **Units** column.

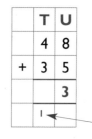

8 + 5 = 13 which is 1 ten and 3 units.
Here's the clever bit: we put the 3 'answer' units in the **Units** column and we **carry** the 1 ten into the **Tens** column.

Note the small carried number here. Written under the line we can check that we have written 13

Tip: Write the carrying digit first and then the answer digit so that you actually write 1 3 in that order.

Step 3:   Now add the digits in the **Tens** column, including the carried number.

	T	U
	4	8
+	3	5
	8	3
	1	

4 + 3 + the carried 1 = 8
Put the 8 'answer' digit in the **Tens** column.

So 48 + 35 = 83

Use Exercise 3.4 to practise this formal way of adding numbers. Take care to set out your work carefully.

Exercise 3.4: Formal addition with carrying

Calculate:

1.
```
      T  U
      2  4
   +  3  8
   _____
```

2.
```
      T  U
      5  6
   +  2  7
   _____
```

3.
```
      T  U
      1  8
   +  7  7
   _____
```

4. 37 + 39

5. 15 + 28

6. 39 + 16

7. 48 + 29

8. 16 + 66

9. 37 + 54

10. 49 + 45

11. 52 + 19

12. 25 + 66

13. 49 + 14

14. 27 + 29

15. 31 + 49

16. 65 + 27

17. 48 + 14

18. 13 + 59

19. 78 + 19

20. 46 + 27

Sometimes we need to carry a number into the **Hundreds** column.
Here are two examples.

Examples:

(i)   48 + 75

Step 1:   First set out the digits in their correct columns.

Step 2:   Then add the digits in the **Units** column.

```
      T  U
      4  8
   +  7  5
   _____
         3
   _____
      1
```

8 + 5 = 13 which is 1 ten and 3 units.
Put the 3 'answer' units in the **Units** column and
carry the 1 ten into the **Tens** column.

Step 3: Now add the digits in the tens column, including the carried digit.

	H	T	U
		4	8
+		7	5
	1	2	3
		1	

4 + 7 + the carried 1 is 12
Put the 2 'answer' digit in the **Tens** column and the 1 hundred into a new **Hundreds** column.

So 48 + 75 = 123

(ii) 83 + 69

	H	T	U
		8	3
+		6	9
	1	5	2
		1	

Note: Sometimes the carrying digit is more than 1
For example, 6 + 9 + 8 = 23
Here the carrying digit is 2

Exercise 3.5: Carrying into the Hundreds column

Calculate:

1. (a)

	H	T	U
		5	4
+		4	7

(b)

	H	T	U
		9	9
+			4

(c)

	H	T	U
		7	8
+		6	6

(d)

	H	T	U
		8	7
+		7	9

(e)

	H	T	U
		6	6
+		4	6

2.

H	T	U
	8	1
+	4	3

3.

H	T	U
	5	7
+	6	5

4.

H	T	U
	9	6
+	5	8

5. 93 + 39

6. 27 + 78

7. What is the sum of 85 and 63?

8. Add together 47 and 79

9. 82 plus 28

10. What is 35 more than 38?

11. How many do 74 and 45 make altogether?

Extension questions:

12. 36 + 89 + 18

13. 45 + 47 + 61

14. 72 + 55 + 26

15. 39 + 27 + 15

16. 55 + 65 + 75

17. 84 + 17 + 29

18. 36 + 79 + 18

19. 54 + 43 + 28

20. 63 + 17 + 89

21. 34 + 98 + 78

22. 74 + 29 + 78

23. 83 + 29 + 17

24. 83 + 74 + 29

25. 76 + 48 + 83

26. 75 + 49 + 26

27. 83 + 74 + 58

28. 14 + 98 + 6

29. 88 + 7 + 28

30. 9 + 38 + 96

When one or both of the numbers is more than 100, you do the same thing, but you need an extra column – the **Hundreds** column.

Examples:

(i) 392 + 147

H	T	U
	3	9	2
+	1	4	7
	5	3	9
	1		

(ii) 467 + 83

H	T	U
	4	6	7
+		8	3
	5	5	0
	1	1	

Exercise 3.6: Adding Hundreds

Calculate these:

1.

H	T	U
	2	8	4
+	1	9	2

2.

H	T	U
	1	9	7
+	5	8	5

3.

H	T	U
	3	4	5
+	2	8	5

4. 281 + 264

5. 648 + 196

6. The sum of 793 and 149

7. 462 plus 186

8. Increase 733 by 178

9. What is 275 more than 378?

10. The total of 396 and 259

11. 382 + 96

12. 87 + 117

13. 126 + 87 + 9

14. 436 + 7 + 82

15. 74 + 194 + 65

Problem solving

When solving a problem you must write down the calculation you are doing. It also helps if you use a few words to explain what the numbers mean.

> **Example:**
>
> A group of people go on holiday to Spain. 27 stay at the Miramar Hotel and 18 stay at the Splendido Hotel. How many people are there in the group?
>
> Number in the group is 27 + 18 = 45

Exercise 3.7: Problem solving

1. A fruit bowl has 5 apples and 8 bananas in it. How many pieces of fruit are there altogether?

2. There are 28 passengers on a bus. 7 more passengers get on at the first stop. How many passengers are there on the bus after the stop?

3. The school secretary uses 18 1st class stamps and 25 2nd class stamps. How many stamps does she use altogether?

4. There are 47 shops on one side of Main Street and 39 on the other side. What is the total number of shops in Main Street?

5. Adam plants 150 tulip bulbs in the flower beds and 85 in pots. How many bulbs does he plant in total?

6. It is 413 miles from London to Edinburgh and 47 miles from Edinburgh to Glasgow. How far is it if someone goes from London to Glasgow through Edinburgh?

7. 124 people are staying at The Regal Hotel and 118 at The Royal Hotel. What is the total number of people staying at the two hotels?

8. In his exams Krishna scores 87 in English, 79 in maths and 71 in science. What is his total mark for all three subjects?

9. Pat collects stamps. He has been given 115 French stamps, 29 Swiss stamps and 8 from Italy. How many stamps has Pat been given?

10. A sweet jar contains 125 peppermints, 84 toffees and 53 jellies. How many sweets are there in the jar?

11. At Barrel Hall there are 128 children in the Senior School, 97 in the Middle School and 139 in the Kindergarten. How many children are there at Barrel Hall?

12. Mrs Bunn rings the baker to order 8 large cakes, 144 buns and 96 jam tarts. How many items will the baker deliver?

13. The numbers 7, 8, 21, 27, 33 and 49 appear on Penny's lottery ticket. What is the sum of these numbers?

14. Adam, Bill and Colin each think of a number. Adam thinks of 85 and Bill's number is 49. Colin does a bit of mental arithmetic and says his number is 16 more than the sum of the other two. What is Colin's number?

15. Ali and Mo own two cars each. The numbers on Ali's number plates are 387 and 496. Mo has the numbers 596 and 289 on her number plates. Whose numbers add up to the larger total? (Hint: This is a two-stage question.)

. . . .

Summary

Often, if you think about the numbers, you will be able to add in your head.

Examples:

(i) 43 + 78   Think of 43 as (40 + 3)

                                and   78 as (70 + 8)

Add the larger numbers together first, and then the smaller ones:

70 + 40 + 3 + 8 = 110 + 11

                = 121

(ii) 53 + 54   Use doubles.

(53 × 2) + 1 = 106 + 1

            = 107

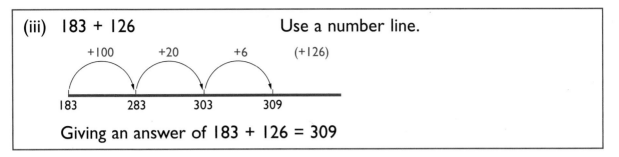

(iii) 183 + 126   Use a number line.

+100   +20   +6   (+126)

183   283   303   309

Giving an answer of 183 + 126 = 309

It does not matter if you have a different way of arriving at an answer. Use the method you find easiest.

For some problems, you might need to use the more formal method we saw on pages 23-30. Just remember to start by setting out the sum with the digits in the correct columns. Here is one more example.

Example: 378 + 6 + 57

Step 1:   Set out the sum with the digits in the correct columns.

	H	T	U
	3	7	8
			6
+		5	7

Step 2:   Add the **Units** column.

	H	T	U
	3	7	8
			6
+		5	7
			1
		2	

(8 + 6 + 7 = 21)
(Write 21 as **2** carried to **Tens** column and 1 in the **Units** column)

Step 3: Repeat with the **Tens** and **Hundreds** columns.

	H	T	U
	3	7	8
			6
+		5	7
	4	4	1
	1	2	

7 + 5 carried 2 = 14
3 + carried 1 = 4

Exercise 3.8: Summary exercise

Try to answer Q1–5 in your head. Make sure you can explain what you did.

1. 34 + 65

2. Add 47 and 8 together.

3. Find the sum of 29 and 56

4. 67 plus 81

5. Increase 96 by 4

You might find Q6-15 easier if you use jottings on a number line. Here's an example to remind you of how a number line works:

Example: 448 + 142

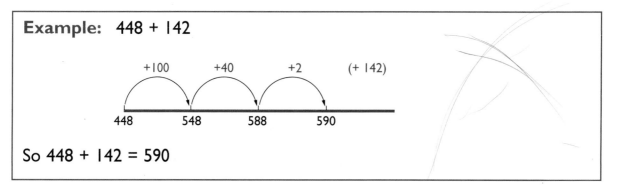

So 448 + 142 = 590

6. 362 + 178

7. 739 + 185

8. 657 + 246

9. 192 + 374

10. 433 + 482

11. 382 + 157

12. 576 + 248

13. 382 + 267 + 194

14. 46 + 527 + 57

15. 198 + 7 + 59

End of chapter activity: Doubles in the 1 to 20 addition chart

1. Make and complete an addition square for the numbers 1 to 20.

2. Shade in the 'doubles' squares.   2 = (1 + 1)

    4 = (2 + 2)

    6 = (3 + 3) and so on . . .

3. Try to learn as many of the doubles as possible.

Did you know?

The **= sign** ('equals sign') was invented by 16th Century Welsh mathematician Robert Recorde, who was fed up with writing 'is equal to' in his equations!

The symbol '=' was not immediately popular. The symbol '||' was used by some people who didn't like it and *ae* (or *oe*) from the Latin word *aequalis* meaning equal was used by others.

Chapter 4: Subtraction

In this chapter we are going to look at subtraction, which you have already met in Chapter 2. There is more about subtraction in Chapter 25: Mental strategies.

Subtraction means finding the difference between two numbers. The difference means what must be added to the smaller number to make the larger number.

Example:	$9 - 4 = ?$
	You can work this out by asking: 'What do I need to add to 4 in order to make 9?'
	You must add 5 to 4 to make 9 $(4 + 5 = 9)$
	So $9 - 4 = 5$

Exercise 4.1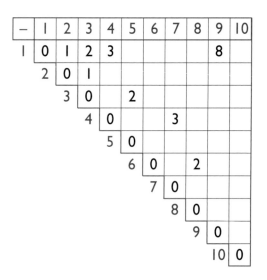

1. Copy and complete this subtraction square. Work along each line, subtracting the number on the left **from** the number at the top.

−	1	2	3	4	5	6	7	8	9	10
1	0	1	2	3					8	
2		0	1							
3			0		2					
4				0			3			
5					0					
6						0		2		
7							0			
8								0		
9									0	
10										0

These calculations are called **subtraction bonds**. It is important to learn all of these by heart because $7 - 4$ is not the same as $4 - 7$

Subtraction from ten

It can be very helpful to learn these subtractions:

$10 - 1 = 9$

$10 - 2 = 8$

$10 - 3 = 7$

$10 - 4 = 6$

$10 - 5 = 5$

$10 - 6 = 4$

$10 - 7 = 3$

$10 - 8 = 2$

$10 - 9 = 1$

Look at how this helps with a calculation like $15 - 8$

Example:	$15 - 8 = (10 + 5) - 8$	Think of 15 as 10 + 5
	$= 10 - 8 + 5$	Rearrange this calculation to take 8 away from 10 and then add the 5
	$= 2 + 5$	
	$= 7$	

Exercise 4.2: Using subtraction from ten

Calculate:

1. $11 - 6$

2. $15 - 9$

3. $13 - 7$

4. $14 - 5$

5. $13 - 6$

6. $16 - 7$

7. $12 - 4$

8. $11 - 3$

9. $15 - 6$

10. $14 - 9$

11.	11 – 7	16.	17 – 8
12.	15 – 8	17.	13 – 9
13.	13 – 8	18.	14 – 7
14.	12 – 7	19.	16 – 9
15.	14 – 6	20.	12 – 5

21.	18 – 9	26.	16 – 8
22.	14 – 8	27.	11 – 2
23.	13 – 5	28.	15 – 7
24.	11 – 9	29.	12 – 8
25.	13 – 4	30.	17 – 9

We can also use this method of subtracting with larger two-digit numbers.

Example:	$27 - 8 = (20 + 7) - 8$	Think of 27 as 20 + 7
	$= 20 - 8 + 7$	Then subtract 8 from 20 to make 12
	$= 12 + 7$	Then add 7 and 12
	$= 19$	

Exercise 4.3: More practice in using subtraction from ten

Calculate:

1. (a) 21 – 4   (f) 27 – 8

    (b) 33 – 7   (g) 31 – 3

    (c) 42 – 5   (h) 22 – 8

    (d) 34 – 6   (i) 26 – 9

    (e) 45 – 7   (j) 46 – 8

(k) 35 – 6

(l) 54 – 9

(m) 51 – 7

(n) 23 – 9

(o) 26 – 8

(p) 52 – 4

(q) 36 – 7

(r) 53 – 8

(s) 41 – 5

(t) 53 – 6

2. (a) 65 – 8

(b) 71 – 6

(c) 97 – 9

(d) 64 – 8

(e) 83 – 4

(f) 104 – 5

(g) 61 – 9

(h) 72 – 7

(i) 100 – 7

(j) 105 – 9

(k) 92 – 3

(l) 82 – 6

(m) 78 – 9

(n) 64 – 7

(o) 81 – 8

(p) 93 – 5

(q) 62 – 9

(r) 91 – 2

(s) 102 – 6

(t) 74 – 5

There are lots of other methods you can use when subtracting in your head. No method is right or wrong – you should use the one you find easiest.

Use Exercise 4.4 to practise subtracting in your head. Then discuss what you did with the rest of your class. You will probably find that each question can be worked out in many different ways. Do any of your classmates use methods you hadn't thought of? Which methods do you prefer?

Exercise 4.4: Subtracting in your head

Do these questions in your head, only writing down little notes. Make sure you can explain what you have done.

> **Tip:** Remember the other words for subtraction: **minus**, **take away** and **less**.

1. 31 – 26

2. 45 minus 27

3. Subtract 6 from 15

4. From 43 subtract 19

5. Take 26 from 50

6. From 56 take 47

7. 21 subtract 6

8. 60 take 43

9. What is the difference between 74 and 47?

10. How many more is 83 than 61?

11. What must be added to 47 to make 63?

12. How many less than 106 is 88?

13. Decrease 53 by 17

14. Alec thinks of a number, adds 17 to it and the result is 50. What number did he think of?

15. What must be subtracted from 96 to make 69?

Subtraction by decomposition

We have already seen how numbers can be broken down to make a subtraction easier to work out. When the numbers are quite large, it helps to set the calculation out in columns.

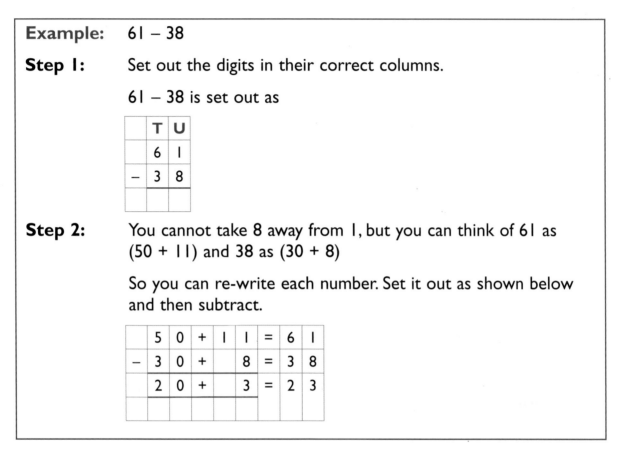

Example: 61 − 38

Step 1: Set out the digits in their correct columns.

61 − 38 is set out as

	T	U
	6	1
−	3	8

Step 2: You cannot take 8 away from 1, but you can think of 61 as (50 + 11) and 38 as (30 + 8)

So you can re-write each number. Set it out as shown below and then subtract.

	5	0	+	1	1	=	6	1
−	3	0	+		8	=	3	8
	2	0	+		3	=	2	3

Exercise 4.5: Subtraction by decomposition

Calculate:

1. 42 − 18
2. 73 − 29
3. 95 − 38
4. 71 − 43
5. 32 − 17

6. 62 − 15
7. 84 − 37
8. 90 − 24
9. 54 − 27
10. 41 − 18

The formal method of subtraction

As we saw in the previous chapter, there is a formal way of setting out calculations. You already know how to do addition using this method – now let's look at subtraction.

Example: 67 – 25

Step 1:   Set out the digits in the correct columns.

67 – 25 is set out as:

T	U
6	7
– 2	5

Step 2:   First subtract the digits in the **Units** column, then subtract the digits in the **Tens** column.

T	U
6	7
– 2	5
4	2

First the units: 7 – 5 = 2
Second the tens: 6 – 2 = 4

Exercise 4.6: Using the formal method of subtraction

Use the formal method to calculate:

1.   94 – 63

2.   78 – 56

3.   49 – 17

4.   82 – 51

5.   63 – 22

6.   95 – 64

7.   56 – 43

8.   27 – 24

9.   69 – 14

10. 85 – 25

11. 233 – 130

12. 863 – 462

13. 935 – 723

14. 782 – 671

15. 524 – 413

16. 450 – 130

17. 246 – 31

18. 174 – 52

19. 787 – 65

20. 148 – 27

In the next example we have to deal with a situation where **the digit we are subtracting from is smaller than the digit being subtracted**.

Example: 73 – 28

Step 1: Set out the digits in the correct columns.

73 – 28 is set out as:

	T	U
	7	3
–	2	8

Step 2: Look at the **Units** column first. You need to subtract 8 from 3 but 8 is larger than 3. So how do you do it? Somehow, the 3 must be made larger. We do this by taking 1 ten from the **Tens** column. This leaves 6 tens in the **Tens** column, so cross out the 7 and write 6 above it. We add the carried ten to the 3 in the **Units** column and we get 10 + 3 = 13. Now we can subtract: 13 – 8 = 5

	T	U
	$^6\cancel{7}$	^{1}3
–	2	8
		5

Step 3: Now subtract the digits in the **Tens** column. Remember that we now have only 6 tens: 6 – 2 = 4

	T	U
	$^6\cancel{7}$	^{1}3
–	2	8
	4	5

Exercise 4.7: More subtraction

Use either a formal method or do the working in your head. You may make rough notes. Make sure you can explain what you did.

1. 42 – 17

2. 91 – 46

3. 70 – 28

4. 81 – 36

5. 31 – 19

6. 85 – 58

7. 63 – 49

8. 52 – 37

9. 95 – 26

10. 31 – 13

11. 64 – 27

12. 41 – 25

13. 92 – 46

14. 94 – 77

15. 84 – 56

16. 82 – 66

17. 97 – 49

18. 56 – 37

19. 48 – 19

20. 57 – 28

The inverse or opposite

- **Addition** is the inverse (**opposite**) of **subtraction**.

- **Subtraction** is the **inverse** of **addition**.

It is important to understand the connection between addition and subtraction.

If you know that:

    3 + 1 = 4   and   1 + 3 = 4

then you also know (because of the rule above) that:

    4 – 3 = 1   and   4 – 1 = 3

Exercise 4.8: Inverses and opposites

Copy these calculations and complete them by putting the missing number in the box.

1. (a) $5 + 3 = \square$

    (b) $\square + 5 = 8$

    (c) $8 - \square = 3$

    (d) $8 - \square = 5$

2. (a) $9 + 5 = \square$

    (b) $\square + 9 = 14$

    (c) $14 - \square = 9$

    (d) $14 - \square = 5$

3. (a) $7 + 8 = \square$

    (b) $\square + 7 = 15$

    (c) $15 - \square = 8$

    (d) $\square - 8 = 7$

4. (a) $5 + \square = 11$

    (b) $\square - 5 = 6$

    (c) $11 - \square = 5$

5. (a) $\square - 2 = 6$

    (b) $\square - 6 = 2$

    (c) $2 + \square = 8$

6. $\square + 8 = 12$

7. $14 + \square = 20$

8. $\square - 2 = 6$

9. $12 - \square = 5$

10. $\square - 3 = 8$

11. $17 + 6 = \square$

12. $\square - 4 = 19$

13. $23 - \square = 17$

14. $13 + 7 = \square$

15. $13 - \square = 9$

16. $\square - 7 = 5$

17. $6 + \square = 15$

18. $\square - 6 = 9$

19. $15 - \square = 6$

20. $\square - 6 = 15$

Here is a slightly more challenging example:

$25 + 12 = 37$ and $12 + 25 = 37$

So we also know that:

$37 - 25 = 12$ and $37 - 12 = 25$

Exercise 4.9:
More practice in inverses and opposites

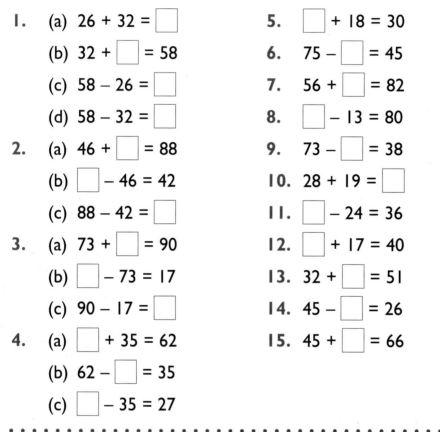

Copy these calculations and complete them by putting the missing number in the box.

1. (a) 26 + 32 = ☐

    (b) 32 + ☐ = 58

    (c) 58 – 26 = ☐

    (d) 58 – 32 = ☐

2. (a) 46 + ☐ = 88

    (b) ☐ – 46 = 42

    (c) 88 – 42 = ☐

3. (a) 73 + ☐ = 90

    (b) ☐ – 73 = 17

    (c) 90 – 17 = ☐

4. (a) ☐ + 35 = 62

    (b) 62 – ☐ = 35

    (c) ☐ – 35 = 27

5. ☐ + 18 = 30

6. 75 – ☐ = 45

7. 56 + ☐ = 82

8. ☐ – 13 = 80

9. 73 – ☐ = 38

10. 28 + 19 = ☐

11. ☐ – 24 = 36

12. ☐ + 17 = 40

13. 32 + ☐ = 51

14. 45 – ☐ = 26

15. 45 + ☐ = 66

Checking your answers

You can use the idea of the inverse to check subtraction.

Examples:	(i)	3 – 1 = 2
		if **2 + 1 = 3** your answer is correct!
	(ii)	76 – 24 = **52**
		if **52 + 24 = 76** your answer is correct!

Exercise 4.10: Checking calculations

Using the method described above, write down whether these calculations are right or wrong.

1. (a) 7 – 4 = 3
    (b) 5 – 1 = 4
    (c) 9 – 6 = 3
    (d) 8 – 5 = 4
    (e) 9 – 4 = 6

    (f) 10 – 7 = 3
    (g) 11 – 4 = 8
    (h) 13 – 3 = 11
    (i) 17 – 5 = 12
    (j) 16 – 8 = 9

    (k) 18 – 9 = 9
    (l) 14 – 6 = 6
    (m) 16 – 9 = 5
    (n) 12 – 7 = 5
    (o) 13 – 8 = 5

    (p) 24 – 13 = 11
    (q) 26 – 11 = 15
    (r) 25 – 12 = 13
    (s) 27 – 19 = 8
    (t) 29 – 14 = 5

2. (a) 84 – 67 = 23
    (b) 73 – 58 = 15
    (c) 92 – 45 = 57
    (d) 63 – 19 = 44
    (e) 81 – 27 = 54

    (f) 37 – 26 = 11
    (g) 48 – 23 = 15
    (h) 53 – 27 = 26
    (i) 69 – 46 = 23
    (j) 83 – 29 = 54

    (k) 78 – 55 = 33
    (l) 90 – 46 = 54
    (m) 50 – 17 = 33
    (n) 65 – 27 = 38
    (o) 41 – 28 = 13

    (p) 146 – 63 = 83
    (q) 150 – 85 = 65
    (r) 128 – 75 = 83
    (s) 196 – 142 = 54
    (t) 200 – 86 = 126

More subtraction

Let us look at how we can use the same formal method as before when there are more than two columns.

Example: 742 – 289

Step 1: First subtract the units column.

H	T	U
7	$^3\cancel{4}$	$^1 2$
– 2	8	9
		3

You cannot subtract 9 from 2 so you need to take 1 ten from the **Tens** column. This leaves 3 tens in the **Tens** column and gives 12 units. Now you can subtract: 12 – 9 = 3

Step 2: Now move on to the **Tens** and **Hundreds** columns.

H	T	U
$^6\cancel{7}$	$^{13}\cancel{4}$	$^1 2$
– 2	8	9
4	5	3

Again you can't take 8 away from 3. So you take 1 from the **Hundreds** column to leave 6 hundreds. You now have 13 tens: 13 – 8 = 5
In the **Hundreds** column: 6 – 2 = 4

If there are zeros in the top line, be extra careful. It can be hard to see what to exchange, you cannot take 1 away from nought. You have to keep going to the left until you find a whole number, then take 1 away from that. Here is an example:

Example: 600 – 286

Step 1: First consider the units column.

H	T	U
$^5\cancel{6}$	$^1 0$	0
– 2	8	6

You cannot subtract 6 from 0, so look at the tens column. There are no tens to borrow, so look at the hundreds. Take 1 from the **Hundreds** column to give 5 hundreds and 10 tens.

Step 2:   Now we can subtract.

H	T	U
^{5}6̸	^{9}0̸	^{1}0
− 2	8	6
3	1	4

Now you can take 1 from the **Tens** column, which leaves 9 tens and gives 10 units.

Subtract: Units $10 - 6 = 4$
Tens $9 - 8 = 1$
Hundreds $5 - 2 = 3$

Exercise 4.11: More subtraction

Calculate (do not forget to check your answers):

1. 853 − 721
2. 374 − 168
3. 550 − 87
4. 821 − 179
5. 317 − 196
6. 513 − 28
7. 407 − 125
8. 347 − 276

9.   705 − 528
10. 320 − 186
11. 500 − 274
12. 908 − 163
13. 742 − 475
14. 342 − 179
15. 700 − 78

Problem solving

Example:

120 children attend swimming lessons at the local pool.
If 67 of them are boys, how many girls have swimming lessons?

Number of girls is 120 − 67 = 53

Exercise 4.12: Problem solving

1. Sara is 4 years younger than Peter, who is 9 years old. How old is Sara?

2. There are 8 apples in a fruit bowl. 5 of them are eaten at lunch. How many apples are left uneaten?

3. Richard starts the term with a box of 12 pencils. At the end of term there are 7 pencils left in the box. How many pencils did Richard use during the term?

4. A maths test is marked out of 20. William loses 13 marks. How many marks did William score?

5. Ali gets 18 marks out of 25 in a science test. How many marks does Ali lose?

6. Fatima cycles to visit her aunt, who lives 12 kilometres away. She stops for a rest after cycling 7 kilometres. How much further has Fatima to cycle to reach her aunt?

7. In a group of 15 girls, 9 of them wear a hairband. How many girls do not wear a hairband?

8. A box of sweets contains either toffees or chocolates. There are 24 sweets altogether, of which 15 are toffees. How many chocolates are there in the box?

9. There are 25 chapters in the book Gigi is reading. She has read the first 7 chapters. How many more chapters has Gigi left to read?

10. A gym club has 30 members, of whom 17 have obtained their primary badge. How many members have not got their primary badge?

11. Miss Total orders 75 new books but only 42 are sent. How many books are still needed?

12. In an exam George scores 29 marks less than Ali, who gets 83 marks. How many marks does George get?

13. The Emperor Hadrian was born in 76AD and died in 138AD. How old was he when he died?

14. At Barrel Hall there are 87 girls and 105 boys. How many more boys are there than girls?

15. Ann has read the first 187 pages of a book which is 274 pages long. How many more pages must Ann read to finish the book?

16. Aleford won their cricket match against Cokeville by 107 runs. Aleford were all out for 350. How many runs did Cokeville score?

17. There are 300 loaves on the bakery shelves when it opens. At closing time there are 38 loaves left. How many loaves have been sold during the day?

18. In the Parliament of Funrovia there are 327 members of the Happy Party and 148 members of the Sad Party. How many more Happy members are there than Sad members?

19. Noel buys 200 stamps and uses 147 of them to send his Christmas cards. How many stamps are left?

20. Ben drives home from London to Rome via Paris. It is 215 miles from London to Paris and 908 miles altogether from London to Rome. How far is Rome from Paris?

Summary

Often, if you think about the numbers carefully, you will be able to do the subtractions in your head. Here are some of the methods you can use.

Examples:

(i) $43 - 38$

Tip: When the numbers are close like this you can simply count on:

38   39   40   41   42   43

Here you have counted on **5** so the answer to the calculation $43 - 38$ is 5

You must write down the answer like this:

$43 - 38 = 5$

(ii) $71 - 8$

Tip: In this example you can be clever and use '10' to make your calculations easier.

Think of 71 as $61 + 10$, so:

$71 - 8 = 61 + 10 - 8$

$= 61 + 2$

$= 63$

(iii) $93 - 46$

Tip: You can sometimes use multiples of 10 to help.

In this example it would be easier to take away 50 from 93 but 50 is 4 more than 46 so we have to make sure we add 4 back into the calculation.

$93 - 46 = 93 - 50 + 4$

$= 43 + 4$

$= 47$

(iv) 563 – 275

Tip: You can use a number line and make notes to help you keep track of where you are. In this example we will use the inverse rule and say: 'What do we need to add to 275 to reach 563?'

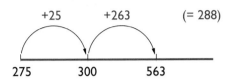

Or we can say: 'What do we need to take away from 563 to reach 275?'

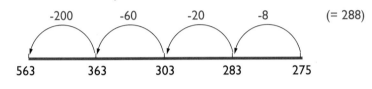

It does not matter if you have a different way of arriving at the answer. If you want to use the more **formal** method, make sure you set your working out clearly. Here are two more examples of the formal method.

Examples:

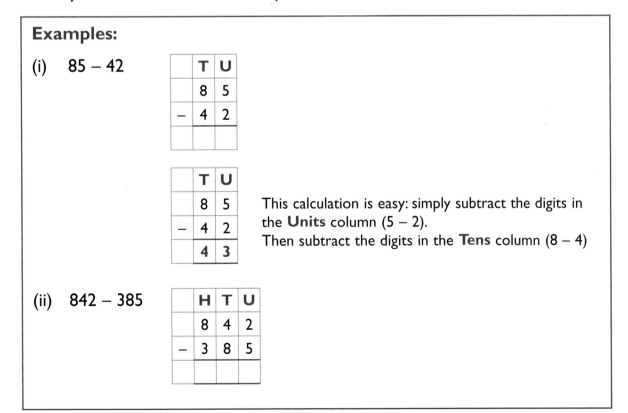

(i) 85 – 42

	T	U
	8	5
–	4	2

	T	U
	8	5
–	4	2
	4	3

This calculation is easy: simply subtract the digits in the **Units** column (5 – 2).
Then subtract the digits in the **Tens** column (8 – 4)

(ii) 842 – 385

	H	T	U
	8	4	2
–	3	8	5

| | | Step 1: | Start with the **Units** column. Since 5 is larger than 2, take 1 from the **Tens** column and add it to the **Units** column to make 12. You can then subtract 5 from 12 |

Step 1: Start with the **Units** column. Since 5 is larger than 2, take 1 from the **Tens** column and add it to the **Units** column to make 12. You can then subtract 5 from 12

H	T	U
8	$^3\cancel{4}$	$^1 2$
− 3	8	5
		7

Step 2: Repeat with **Tens** and then the **Hundreds** columns.

H	T	U
$^7 \cancel{8}$	$^{13}\cancel{4}$	$^1 2$
− 3	8	5
4	5	7

Tip: Remember that addition and subtraction are the **inverse** of each other.

Given that	$43 + 17 = 60$
it follows that	$60 − 43 = 17$
and	$60 − 17 = 43$

You can use this to check your answer to a subtraction. Add the answer and the smaller number together. Their sum should be the larger number.

Exercise 4.13: Summary exercise

Try to answer Q1–10 in your head. Make sure you can explain what you did.

1. $9 − 4$
2. $17 − 8$
3. $12 − 4$
4. $27 − 13$
5. $31 − 24$
6. $89 − 82$
7. $61 − 7$
8. $45 − 36$
9. $72 − 25$
10. $85 − 48$

You might want to use a number line to help you answer Q11–20. Here is an example of a number line subtraction to remind you what to do:

Example:

(i)   31 – 24

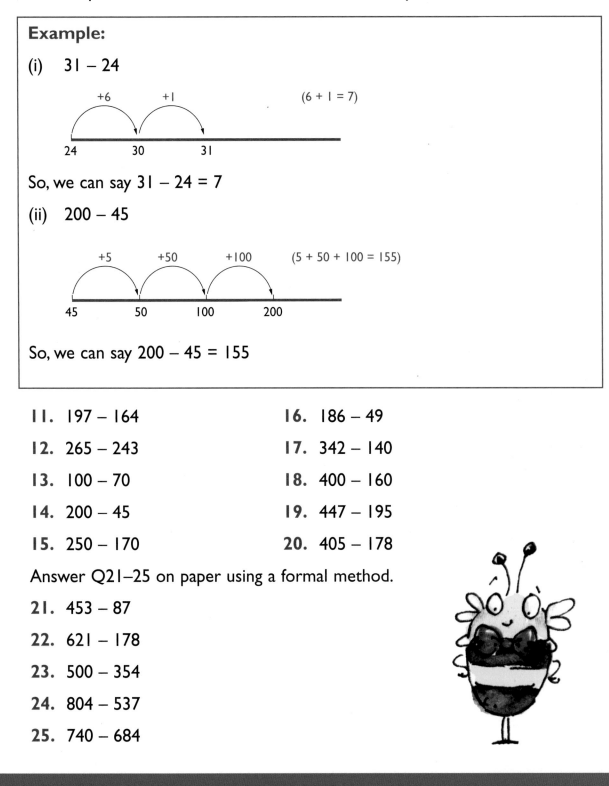

+6   +1   (6 + 1 = 7)

24   30   31

So, we can say 31 – 24 = 7

(ii)   200 – 45

+5   +50   +100   (5 + 50 + 100 = 155)

45   50   100   200

So, we can say 200 – 45 = 155

11. 197 – 164   16. 186 – 49

12. 265 – 243   17. 342 – 140

13. 100 – 70   18. 400 – 160

14. 200 – 45   19. 447 – 195

15. 250 – 170   20. 405 – 178

Answer Q21–25 on paper using a formal method.

21. 453 – 87

22. 621 – 178

23. 500 – 354

24. 804 – 537

25. 740 – 684

For Q26–30, write down the number that should replace the asterisk (*).

26. 57 + 26 = *

27. 83 – * = 26

28. 83 – * = 57

29. * – 16 = 51

30. 112 – * = 89

End of chapter activity: Subtraction chart

1. Make a subtraction chart like the one at the beginning of the chapter (page 36). Make it large enough to find the difference between all numbers from 1 to 20.

2. Try to learn as many of them as possible.

Did you know?

The tallest living man is Leonid Stadyk of the Ukraine. He is 253 cm (8 ft 3 in) tall!

The smallest living man is Lin Yin-Chih of Taipan, Taiwan. He is $67\frac{1}{2}$ cm (2 ft 3 in) tall!

Can you work out how much taller Leonid is than Lin Yin-Chih?

Chapter 5: Addition and subtraction

The + (plus) and − (minus) signs are instructions. They tell us what to do with the number that **follows** the sign. They are like road signs that tell us what is coming next and what we are meant to do.

Examples:

(i) The calculation 42 + 15 − 29 means

- start with 42
- then add 15
- and then subtract 29

This gives the answer 28

Here's the formal way of writing this down:

	T	U
	4	2
+	1	5
	5	7
−	2	9
	2	8

(ii) 46 − 18 + 54 means

- start with 46
- then subtract 18
- and finally add 54

	T	U
	4	6
−	1	8
	2	8
+	5	4
	8	2

Exercise 5.1: Addition and subtraction

Calculate:

1. $7 + 2 - 5$
2. $9 - 6 + 4$
3. $12 - 7 + 3$
4. $13 - 8 + 7$
5. $7 + 8 - 4$

6. $6 + 7 - 8$
7. $13 + 11 - 8$
8. $17 - 9 + 6$
9. $24 + 6 - 17$
10. $40 - 35 + 8$

Extension questions:

11. $24 + 31 - 42$
12. $82 + 73 - 127$
13. $63 - 57 + 38$
14. $85 - 68 + 49$
15. $98 + 42 - 86$

16. $278 - 157 + 324$
17. $428 + 329 - 278$
18. $106 + 364 - 275$
19. $516 - 98 + 427$
20. $765 - 270 - 187$

Problem solving

You learnt in Chapters 3 and 4 that when you solve a problem, whether you are solving it in your head or working on paper, you must write down what you are doing. It also helps if you use a few words to explain what the numbers mean.

Example:

Gwen and Helen bring biscuits to school. Gwen brings 12 biscuits and Helen 18. After each member of the class has eaten one biscuit there are 7 biscuits left. How many children are there in the class?

Always read this sort of question carefully. We can start by working out how many biscuits Gwen and Helen bring to school:

Number of biscuits is $12 + 18 = 30$

We are then told that everyone in the class eats one biscuit and that there are 7 left. We can now work out how many children there are:

$30 - 7 = 23$

We now know that there are 23 children in the class.

We can write this as one calculation:

Number of children is $12 + 18 - 7 = 23$

Exercise 5.2: Problem solving

1. There are 8 apples in a bowl. Liam eats 1 apple and Nicola eats 2 apples.

    (a) How many apples do Liam and Nicola eat altogether?

    (b) How many apples are left in the bowl?

2. A coach goes from London to Portsmouth with one stop at Guildford. There are 33 passengers on board when it leaves London. 7 people get off at Guildford.

    (a) How many people are left on the coach?

    17 people then get on the coach.

    (b) How many passengers travel to Portsmouth?

3. In the Junior School there are 3 forms. J1 has 15 children, J2 has 9 children and there are 17 children in J3.

    (a) How many children are there altogether in the Junior School?

    Each child needs a new maths book but the teacher has only 30 copies.

    (b) How many more books will she need?

4. The school secretary has 58 1st class stamps and 76 2nd class stamps in her office.

    (a) How many stamps does she have altogether?

On Friday she uses 24 1st class and 15 2nd class stamps.

(b) How many stamps does she use?

(c) How many stamps does she have left?

5. A book is 250 pages long and is divided into three parts. Part one is 39 pages long and there are 117 pages in part two.

   (a) What is the total number of pages in parts one and two?

   (b) How many pages are there in part three?

6. Three friends share a box of 72 chocolates. Harry takes 12, Jane takes 9 and Mandy has 18.

   How many chocolates are left?

7. Ramon is trying to score 301 on a dart board. He scores 89, 117 and then 67.

   How many more must he score to get to 301?

8. A Christmas decoration in the High Street has 720 flashing lights which are either red, white, green or blue.

   185 are red, 175 are white and 165 are green.

   How many blue lights are there?

9. Arthur has 80 bananas to give to his monkeys. On Monday he gives them 22; he gives them 19 on Tuesday.

   (a) How many bananas are left on Wednesday morning?

   (b) How many more bananas must he buy so that he has 100 in stock for the rest of the week?

10. In a maths test Rachel gets 2 marks for every correct answer, loses 1 mark for every wrong answer and gets no marks for a question she does not answer. Rachel answers 12 questions correctly, gets five questions wrong and leaves out three questions.

    What is Rachel's final mark?

Summary

Remember: the 'sign' **rules** the number that **follows** it.

Examples:

(i) $4 + 10 - 3$ Start at 4, then add 10 to make 14, then subtract 3 from the 14 to get the answer 11

(ii) $36 + 10 - 12$ Start at 36, then add 10 to make 46, then subtract 12 to get the answer 34

(iii) $48 - 16 + 31$ Start at 48, then subtract 16 to make 32, then add 31 to get the answer 63

(iv) $64 - 28 - 15$ Start at 64, then subtract 28 to make 36, then subtract 15 to get the answer 21

Exercise 5.3: Summary exercise

Calculate:

1. $7 + 2 - 6$
2. $8 - 6 + 5$
3. $7 + 5 - 8$
4. $9 - 7 + 6$
5. $8 - 3 - 4$
6. $13 + 9 - 6$
7. $14 - 11 + 9$
8. $15 + 7 - 13$
9. $19 - 5 + 7$
10. $18 - 7 - 8$

11. $32 + 48 - 50$
12. $28 - 18 + 32$
13. $47 + 28 - 16$
14. $52 - 17 - 21$
15. $83 - 24 - 39$
16. $43 - 39 + 65$
17. $84 + 71 - 27$
18. $38 + 96 - 42$
19. $95 - 49 - 37$
20. $87 + 75 - 68$

Extension questions:

21.	38 + 97 – 16	31.	102 – 87 + 149
22.	48 + 89 – 31	32.	216 + 143 – 89
23.	46 – 29 + 98	33.	287 – 49 – 163
24.	106 + 42 – 39	34.	342 + 163 – 248
25.	148 – 73 + 52	35.	403 – 89 – 173
26.	45 + 129 – 37	36.	317 + 229 – 148
27.	87 + 42 – 117	37.	503 – 275 + 186
28.	73 + 87 – 125	38.	194 + 397 – 238
29.	183 – 27 – 94	39.	640 – 173 – 419
30.	129 + 93 – 27	40.	273 – 195 + 389

End of chapter activity: Board game

You will need a copy of the board game (available from the Worksheet CD), a die and some counters.

Any number of players can take part.

How to play

1. Put your counter on 0 to start.

2. Throw the die and move the number of spaces it shows.

3. Follow any instructions found on the square you land on. Some squares tell you to add or subtract a number. Calculate the new number and move your counter accordingly.

    For example: Imagine you have landed on 17. The square says '+2', so add 2 to 17 and go forward to 19

    Imagine you have landed on 26. The square says '–5', so go back to 21

4. The winner is the player who reaches the finish line first.

Did you know?

Until the age of fourteen Aztec children were educated by their parents who taught them a lot about their Aztec ancestors.

When they were fifteen all boys and girls went to school. The Aztecs were one of the first people in the world to make all children go to school. There were two types of school: one for studying practical and military studies and another to learn writing, maths, astronomy and so on.

In Chapter 2 (page 19) you saw how they wrote the numbers 1, 20, 400 and 8000. Here are a few other numbers:

2   ••

200

From what you know can you work out what these numbers are?

1.   800

4.   8400

2.   10

5.   420

3.   80

6   600

Chapter 6: Multiplication

In this chapter we are going to look at multiplication. As with addition and subtraction, there are lots of different methods we can use. There is more on multiplication in Chapter 25: Mental strategies.

Multiplication is a quick way to do repeated addition.

Example:

2	= 2	(1 lot of 2)
2 + 2	= 4	(2 lots of 2)
2 + 2 + 2	= 6	(3 lots of 2)
2 + 2 + 2 + 2	= 8	(4 lots of 2)
2 + 2 + 2 + 2 + 2	= 10	(5 lots of 2)
2 + 2 + 2 + 2 + 2 + 2	= 12	(6 lots of 2)

Do you recognise this as the 2 times table?

$1 \times 2 = 2$ (x means 'times' or 'lots of')

$2 \times 2 = 4$

$3 \times 2 = 6$

$4 \times 2 = 8$

$5 \times 2 = 10$

$6 \times 2 = 12$

$7 \times 2 = 14$

$8 \times 2 = 16$

$9 \times 2 = 18$

$10 \times 2 = 20$

$11 \times 2 = 22$

$12 \times 2 = 24$

The **result** of multiplying two numbers together is known as the **product**.

> **Note:** Multiplying by 1 does not change the number. Think about it: 1 lot of 4 is still 4

You can continue the 2 times table for as long as you like. Just keep on adding 2 each time.

$$13 \times 2 = 26 \qquad (24 + 2)$$

$$14 \times 2 = 28 \qquad (26 + 2)$$

$$15 \times 2 = 30 \qquad (28 + 2) \dots \text{and so on.}$$

The **result** of multiplying numbers together is also called a **multiple**.

Example: 6 times 2 = 12

or   6 lots of 2 = 12

or   the 6th **multiple of 2** is 12

> **Tip:** It will help if you know your times tables. Let us spend some time making sure you know your 2, 3, 4, 5, 6 and 10 times tables before we go any further.

2 times table	**3 times table**
1 x 2 = 2	1 x 3 = 3
2 x 2 = 4	2 x 3 = 6
3 x 2 = 6	3 x 3 = 9
4 x 2 = 8	4 x 3 = 12
5 x 2 = 10	5 x 3 = 15
6 x 2 = 12	6 x 3 = 18
7 x 2 = 14	7 x 3 = 21
8 x 2 = 16	8 x 3 = 24
9 x 2 = 18	9 x 3 = 27
10 x 2 = 20	10 x 3 = 30
11 x 2 = 22	11 x 3 = 33
12 x 2 = 24	12 x 3 = 36

4 times table

1 x 4 = 4
2 x 4 = 8
3 x 4 = 12
4 x 4 = 16
5 x 4 = 20
6 x 4 = 24
7 x 4 = 28
8 x 4 = 32
9 x 4 = 36
10 x 4 = 40
11 x 4 = 44
12 x 4 = 48

5 times table

1 x 5 = 5
2 x 5 = 10
3 x 5 = 15
4 x 5 = 20
5 x 5 = 25
6 x 5 = 30
7 x 5 = 35
8 x 5 = 40
9 x 5 = 45
10 x 5 = 50
11 x 5 = 55
12 x 5 = 60

6 times table

1 x 6 = 6
2 x 6 = 12
3 x 6 = 18
4 x 6 = 24
5 x 6 = 30
6 x 6 = 36
7 x 6 = 42
8 x 6 = 48
9 x 6 = 54
10 x 6 = 60
11 x 6 = 66
12 x 6 = 72

10 times table

1 x 10 = 10
2 x 10 = 20
3 x 10 = 30
4 x 10 = 40
5 x 10 = 50
6 x 10 = 60
7 x 10 = 70
8 x 10 = 80
9 x 10 = 90
10 x 10 = 100
11 x 10 = 110
12 x 10 = 120

Note: You may not know all of these now, but by the end of the chapter you should know them well. Do ask someone to help you practise them.

Exercise 6.1: Multiples

1. Look at the multiplication table below. Copy and complete this table by filling it in with these times tables:

   (a) 2 times   (d) 3 times

   (b) 5 times   (e) 4 times

   (c) 10 times   (f) 6 times

×	2	5	10	3	4	6
1						
2						
3						
4						
5						
6						
7						
8						
9						
10						

2. In which tables will you find these multiples?

   (a) 6   9   12   15   (f) 12   24   36   48

   (b) 12   18   24   30   (g) 22   33   44   55

   (c) 24   28   32   36   (h) 20   40   60   80

   (d) 36   38   40   42   (i) 25   50   75   100

   (e) 65   70   75   80   (j) 15   30   45   60

Below are two shapes with different numbers of rows and columns. Look at each one and count how many boxes there are in each.

Example:

(i)

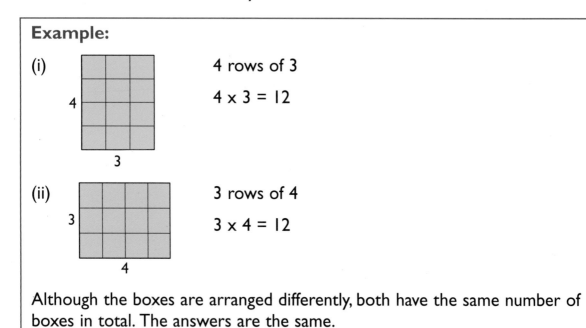

4 rows of 3

4 x 3 = 12

(ii)

3 rows of 4

3 x 4 = 12

Although the boxes are arranged differently, both have the same number of boxes in total. The answers are the same.

This tells us that it does not matter which way round numbers are multiplied together the answer will be the same.

4 x 3 = 12

3 x 4 = 12

Here are some more examples:

If 6 x 2 = 12   then you also know that 2 x 6 = 12
If 4 x 10 = 40 then you also know that 10 x 4 = 40

Learn your tables so that you can remember multiples quickly.

Exercise 6.2: Test yourself

How fast can you answer the following?

1. 7 x 2
2. 4 x 5
3. 6 x 6
4. 8 x 3
5. 6 x 9

6. eight fours
7. nine twos
8. four tens
9. seven sixes
10. five eights

11. 3 times 3
12. 6 times 4
13. 10 times 10
14. 5 times 6
15. 3 times 7

16. 4 multiplied by 4
17. 2 multiplied by 5
18. 7 multiplied by 4
19. 9 multiplied by 5
20. 2 multiplied by 8

21. the product of 5 and 5
22. the product of 9 and 3
23. the product of 2 and 10
24. the product of 4 and 3
25. the product of 6 and 8

26. the 2nd multiple of 3
27. the 7th multiple of 5
28. the 9th multiple of 5
29. the 3rd multiple of 5
30. the 10th multiple of 6

Multiplying by ten and one hundred

When **multiplying by 10** the digits move **1 place** to the left: that is, the **units digit moves** to the **Tens** column.

Examples:

(i) $\quad 5 \times 10 = 50$

(ii) $\quad 81 \times 10 = 810$

(iii) $123 \times 10 = 1230$

When **multiplying by 100** the digits move **2 places** to the left: the **units digit moves** to the **Hundreds** column.

Examples

(i) $\quad 3 \times 100 = 300$

(ii) $\quad 12 \times 100 = 1200$

Exercise 6.3: Multiples of ten and one hundred

Calculate:

1. 17×10

2. 65×10

3. 80×10

4. 148×10

5. 505×10

6. 43×10

7. 68×10

8. 30×10

9. 742×10

10. 300×10

11. 6×100

12. 15×100

13. 30×100

14. 120×100

15. 202×100

16. 74×100

17. 250×100

18. 9×100

19. 60×100

20. 400×100

Multiplication by partition

Partition means separation. We can make multiplications simpler by partitioning one of the numbers.

Example:	40 x 6

We know that   40 = 4 x 10 so we can say:

40 x 6 = 4 x 10 x 6

= 4 x 6 x 10

= 24 x 10

= 240

(Remember: you can multiply in any order, so we can rearrange this to make it easier. We know that 4 x 6 = 24. It is then easy to multiply by 10)

Exercise 6.4: Multiplication by partition

1. 40 x 2
2. 30 x 3
3. 20 x 4
4. 50 x 5
5. 40 x 6

6. 60 x 2
7. 30 x 6
8. 50 x 4
9. 20 x 3
10. 30 x 5

11. 80 x 7
12. 60 x 8
13. 30 x 9
14. 90 x 2
15. 70 x 6

16. 60 x 6
17. 80 x 5
18. 50 x 6
19. 40 x 7
20. 20 x 9

Any number with more than one digit can be partitioned — not just multiples of 10

Example: 37 x 4

Think of 37 as 30 + 7

Multiply both the 30 and the 7 by 4 to find the answer.

$$37 \times 4 = [30 \times 4] + [7 \times 4]$$
$$= 120 + 28$$
$$= 148$$

The formal method of multiplication

Extension topic
We can also use the **formal method** of multiplication. To do this, we set out the calculation in columns, as we did for addition and subtraction in Chapters 3 and 4. Let's look at 37 x 4 again. There are two slightly different ways of doing it.

Example: 37 x 4

Method 1

	H	T	U
		3	7
x			4
		2	8
+	1	2	0
	1	4	8

Step 1: Multiply 7 by 4, the answer is 28. Put the 8 in the **Units** column and the 2 tens in the **Tens** column below the line.

Step 2: Now multiply the 3 tens in the **Tens** column (30) by 4. The answer is 120. Put the digits in the correct columns under the 28

Step 3: Add 28 + 120 = 148

Method 2

When using the formal method, we can **carry** numbers, as we did when adding.

	H	T	U
		3	7
×			4
	1	4	8
		2	

Step 1: 7 x 4 = 28 Put the unit 8 in the **Units** column as before, but **carry** the 2 tens to the **Tens** column, writing it below the line as shown.

Step 2: 3 x 4 = 12 then add the carried 2 to make 14. Put the digits in the correct columns.

Note the small carried number here. Written under the line we can check that we have written 28

Exercise 6.5: Practising partition and the formal method of multiplication

Calculate each of the following. Use (a) partition, the first two questions have been laid out for you, and (b) the formal method of multiplication (for extension work).

1.

	H	T	U
		4	3
×			2
+			

2.

	H	T	U
		8	6
×			3
+			

3. 47 x 4

4. 29 x 5

5. 30 x 4

6. 24 x 6

7. 46 x 5

8. 87 x 4

9. 78 x 2

10. 63 x 6

11. 94 x 2

12. 54 x 4

13. 96 x 3

14. 47 x 4

15. 27 x 5

16. 38 x 6

17. 89 x 4

18. 21 x 8

19. 34 x 7

20. 13 x 9

Problem solving

Remember when solving a problem, whether you are solving it in your head or working on paper, you must write down the calculation you are doing. It also helps if you use a few words to explain what the numbers mean.

Example:

There are 16 coloured pencils in a wallet. How many pencils are there in 4 wallets?

Number of pencils is 16 x 4 = 64

Exercise 6.6: Problem solving

1. There are 48 nails in a packet. How many nails are there altogether in 6 packets?

2. There are 36 peppermints in a tube. What is the total number of peppermints in 3 tubes?

3. Chocolate wafers are packed in boxes of 72. How many wafers are there in 4 boxes?

4. A newspaper has 64 pages. How many pages are there in 10 copies of the newspaper?

5. There are 30 balloons in a bag. How many balloons are there in 5 bags?

6. Eggs are sold in boxes of 6. How many eggs are there in 36 boxes?

7. A large cardboard box contains 48 packets of crisps. How many packets are there in 4 boxes?

8. There are 5 levels in a multi-storey car park. Each level has space for 28 cars. How many cars are there when the car park is full?

9. Mini Christmas crackers are sold in boxes of 24. Sue buys 6 boxes. Will she have enough crackers to give 170 children a cracker each?

10. Paul plays darts. He throws a single 19, a double 17 and a treble 14. What is his total score?

Summary

Make sure you know your 2, 3, 4, 5, 6 and 10 times tables. Test yourself and each other.

> **Remember:**
>
> - When **multiplying by 10** the digits **move 1 place to the left**.
> - When **multiplying by 100** the digits **move 2 places to the left**.

Make sure you can use both methods of multiplication.

Example: 43 x 6

Partition

$$43 \times 6 = (40 \times 6) + (3 \times 6)$$
$$= 240 + 18$$
$$= 258$$

The formal method of multiplication (Extension topic):

(i) Method 1

	H	T	U
		4	3
x			6
		1	8
+	2	4	0
	2	5	8

Step 1: 6 x 3 = 18
Step 2: 6 x 40 = 240
Step 3: 18 + 240 = 258

(ii) Method 2

	H	T	U
		4	3
x			6
	2	5	8
		1	

Step 1: 6 x 3 = 18 Put 8 in **Units** column and carry 1

Step 2: 6 x 4 = 24 plus the carried 1 equals 25

Exercise 6.7: Summary exercise

1. Calculate:

   (a) 4 x 6

   (b) 5 x 6

   (c) multiply 9 by 2

   (d) multiply 4 by 10

   (e) the product of 3 and 6

   (f) the product of 4 and 9

   (g) the 8th multiple of 6

   (h) the 5th multiple of 5

   (i) double 7

   (j) treble 4

2. Calculate:

   (a) 78 x 10

   (b) 38 x 2

   (c) 49 x 3

   (d) 65 x 4

   (e) 87 x 5

   (f) 93 x 6

   (g) 43 x 2

   (h) 52 x 3

   (i) 82 x 4

   (j) 36 x 5

   (k) 77 x 6

   (l) 80 x 4

3. Postage stamps are sold in books of 12. How many stamps are there altogether in 6 books of stamps?

4. Each child is to be given 2 rolls for a picnic. How many rolls are needed if 48 children go on the picnic?

5. A horse needs 4 horseshoes. The blacksmith is asked to give 15 horses new shoes. How many horseshoes are needed altogether?

6. Robert buys 24 cases of wine. There are 6 bottles in each case. How many bottles does Robert buy?

7. To make a fencing panel Arthur needs 27 planks of wood. How many planks does Arthur need to make 3 fencing panels?

8. A number of children is divided up into 4 groups of 36. How many children are there altogether?

9. Farmer Jackson has 5 chicken coops, with 27 hens in each. How many hens does farmer Jackson have?

10. A pencil set contains 2 pencils, a pencil sharpener, an eraser and a ruler. How many items are there altogether in 50 pencil sets?

End of chapter activity: Numbers as rectangles

Numbers can be drawn as rectangles. Any number can be shown as a rectangle measuring the number itself x 1 (see example below).

Example: 5

Since all numbers can be shown like this we will not include them in this activity. But other numbers can be shown in a **different way**.

Example: 6

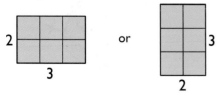

Since 3 x 2 is the same as 2 x 3 these two rectangles count as only one. But some numbers can be shown in more than 1 way (see example on the next page).

Example: 12

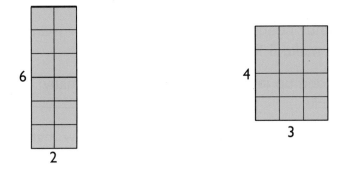

1. On squared paper, draw as many different rectangles as possible to show these numbers:

   14   15   18   20   21   24   30

2. Some numbers can be drawn as squares. On squared paper draw as many square numbers less than 40 as you can (there are six altogether).

. . . .

Did you know?

If you multiply 111 111 111 by 111 111 111 you get 12 345 678 987 654 321

Chapter 7: Division

In this chapter we are going to learn about division, which means finding how many times a number is contained in another number. You can find out more about division in Chapter 25: Mental strategies.

We can think about division in lots of different ways. The following examples show how we can think about how many times 2 goes into 6

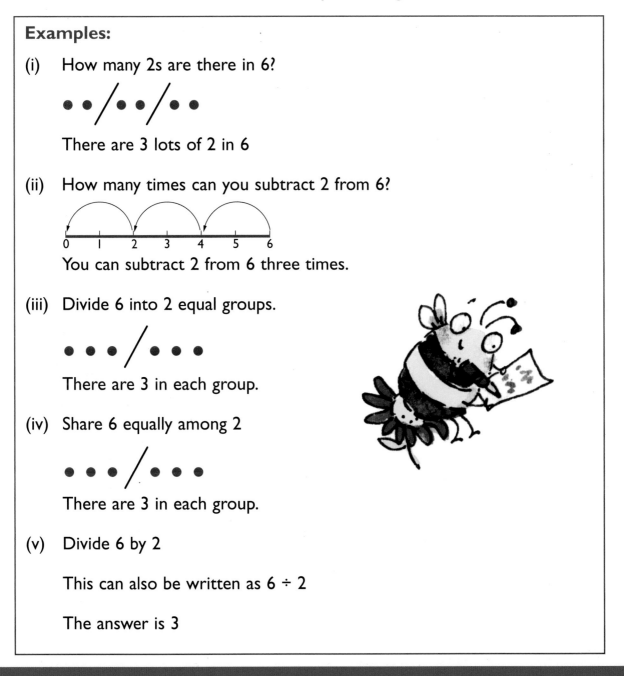

Examples:

(i) How many 2s are there in 6?

There are 3 lots of 2 in 6

(ii) How many times can you subtract 2 from 6?

You can subtract 2 from 6 three times.

(iii) Divide 6 into 2 equal groups.

There are 3 in each group.

(iv) Share 6 equally among 2

There are 3 in each group.

(v) Divide 6 by 2

This can also be written as 6 ÷ 2

The answer is 3

You can use a table chart to work out a division.

Example: Find 6 ÷ 2

Look at the table on the right.

- First find 2 in the left-hand column.
- Then look along the line for 6
- Finally look at the top line above the 6 to find the answer.

6 ÷ 2 = 3

x	1	2	③	4
1	1	2	3	4
②	2	4	⑥	8
3	3	6	9	12
4	4	8	12	16

Exercise 7.1: Easy division

1. Divide:

   (a) 6 by 3

   (b) 18 by 2

   (c) 35 by 5

   (d) 60 by 6

   (e) 48 by 6

   (f) 30 by 10

   (g) 14 by 2

   (h) 27 by 3

   (i) 36 by 4

   (j) 36 by 6

2. Share:

   (a) 20 among 2

   (b) 32 among 4

   (c) 24 among 3

   (d) 24 among 6

   (e) 15 among 5

   (f) 24 among 4

   (g) 42 among 6

   (h) 12 among 2

   (i) 45 among 5

   (j) 18 among 3

3. Work out:

    (a) how many 8s there are in 80

    (b) how many 6s there are in 42

    (c) how many 5s there are in 30

    (d) how many 3s there are in 21

    (e) how many 4s there are in 16

All the answers in Exercise 7.1 are exact. However this is not always the case. Sometimes the answer is not exact, there is something left over, a **remainder**.

Example: 17 ÷ 3

Look at the table below:

×	1	2	3	4	⑤	6
1	1	2	3	4	5	6
2	2	4	6	8	10	12
③	3	6	9	12	⑮	18
4	4	8	12	16	20	24

- Find 3 in the left-hand column.

- Look along the line for the highest number that is less than 17, the 15

- Look at the top line above the 15

17 ÷ 3 = 5 remainder 2   Remainder 2 because 17 − 15 = 2

You could also think of this in terms of having 17 squares and wanting to put them into rows of 3 (write this as 17 ÷ 3) and make 5 rows of 3 with 15 squares and have 2 squares left over.

17 ÷ 3 = 5 remainder 2

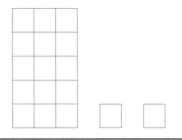

Exercise 7.2: Division with remainders

When you answer the questions in this exercise, remember to write down any remainders.

Divide:

1. 15 by 2
2. 19 by 5
3. 10 by 4
4. 22 by 3
5. 27 by 4
6. 40 by 6
7. 33 by 10
8. 38 by 5
9. 18 by 4
10. 26 by 6

11. 44 by 5
12. 38 by 6
13. 11 by 2
14. 14 by 3
15. 22 by 4
16. 19 by 5
17. 29 by 6
18. 30 by 4
19. 19 by 2
20. 65 by 10

Fractions and division

You have almost certainly come across fractions and division in everyday life, perhaps when you have been asked to share something out, such as a pizza or a bag of sweets. You may have come across the following:

- A half ($\frac{1}{2}$) means that something is divided into 2 equal parts.

- A third ($\frac{1}{3}$) means that something is divided into 3 equal parts. ($\frac{1}{3}$ shaded area)

- A quarter ($\frac{1}{4}$) means that something is divided into 4 equal parts.

  Here are some more interesting ones:

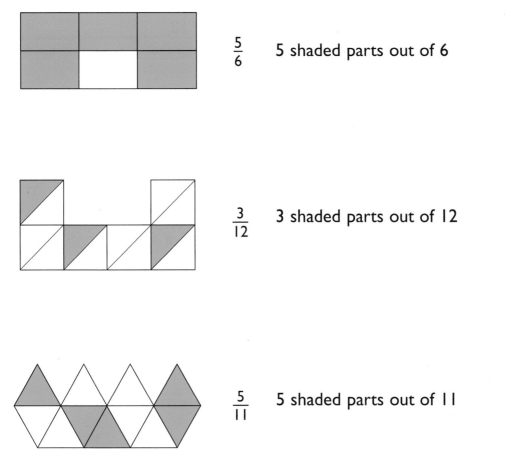

$\frac{5}{6}$ 5 shaded parts out of 6

$\frac{3}{12}$ 3 shaded parts out of 12

$\frac{5}{11}$ 5 shaded parts out of 11

Asking for a fraction of something is really a division calculation in disguise!

Example:	What is a fifth of 35?
	$35 \div 5 = 7$

Exercise 7.3: Fractions and division

Calculate:

1. $\frac{1}{2}$ of 8

2. A quarter of 36

3. $\frac{1}{6}$ of 24

4. One third of 27

5. $\frac{1}{10}$ of 60

6. $\frac{1}{5}$ of 20

7. A half of 18

8. $\frac{1}{4}$ of 20

9. $\frac{1}{3}$ of 18

10. One sixth of 30

11. A tenth of 40

12. One fifth of 40

13. A half of 20

14. $\frac{1}{6}$ of 12

15. One half of 12

16. A quarter of 12

17. One third of 18

18. $\frac{1}{10}$ of 100

19. $\frac{1}{2}$ of 40

20. $\frac{1}{5}$ of 60

Division by ten and one hundred

When **dividing by 10** the digits **move 1 place** to the **right**: the tens digit moves to the **Units** column.

Examples:

(i) $70 \div 10 = 7$ (ii) $500 \div 10 = 50$ (iii) $450 \div 10 = 45$

When **dividing by 100** the digits **move 2 places** to the **right**: the hundreds digit moves to the **Units** column.

Examples:

(i) $600 \div 100 = 6$ (ii) $1200 \div 100 = 12$ (iii) $24\,500 \div 100 = 245$

Exercise 7.4: Division by ten and one hundred

Calculate:

1. $50 \div 10$

2. $200 \div 10$

3. $370 \div 10$

4. $3000 \div 10$

5. $7740 \div 10$

6. $480 \div 10$

7. $600 \div 10$

8. $1490 \div 10$

9. $2300 \div 10$

10. $4040 \div 10$

Extension questions:

11. $900 \div 100$

12. $1400 \div 100$

13. $2000 \div 100$

14. $10\,000 \div 100$

15. $12\,300 \div 100$

16. $1800 \div 100$

17. $900 \div 100$

18. $4900 \div 100$

19. $5000 \div 100$

20. $60\,000 \div 100$

. . . .

The informal method of division

As we saw at the beginning of the chapter, one way of thinking of division is as repeated subtraction.

Examples:

(i) $28 \div 2$

   You know that 10 lots of 2 is 20 so start by seeing how many 20s you can take away from 28

Then you can see how many lots of 2 are left.

	2	8
−	2	0
		8
−		8
	0	0

Take away **10** lots of 2 to leave 8

Now see how many lots of 2 are left. There are **4** lots of 2 in 8 When you reach **00** you have come to the end of your calculation.

So we have calculated that $28 \div 2 = 14$ (10 + 4 = 14 lots of 2)

(ii)   Another way of doing division is by using jumps along a number line.

$20 \div 5$

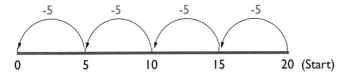

0   5   10   15   20 (Start)

(**4** lots of 5 have been subtracted from 20 to reach 0)

So, $20 \div 5 = 4$

(iii) $92 \div 4$

This time you need to look for lots of 4. Let us look at two methods of doing this.

First method

	9	2
−	4	0
	5	2
−	4	0
	1	2
❼	1	2
	0	0

(**10** lots of 4)

(**10** lots of 4)

(**3** lots of 4)

so, $92 \div 4 = 23$

(10 + 10 + 3 = 23 lots of 4)

Second method

	9	2
−	8	0
	1	2
−	1	2
	0	0

(**20** lots of 4)

(**3** lots of 4)

so, $92 \div 4 = 23$

(20 + 3 = 23 lots of 4)

Exercise 7.5: Informal division

Calculate the following, making notes if you wish (all answers are exact):

1. $34 \div 2$

2. $54 \div 3$

3. $68 \div 4$

4. $75 \div 5$

5. $84 \div 6$

6. $94 \div 2$

7. $48 \div 3$

8. $52 \div 4$

9. $56 \div 2$

10. $69 \div 3$

11. $90 \div 5$

12. $92 \div 4$

13. $72 \div 6$

14. $65 \div 5$

15. $78 \div 6$

The inverse

- Multiplication is the **inverse** (opposite) of division

- Division is the **inverse** of multiplication

It is important to understand the connection between multiplication and division.

If you know that: $\qquad$ $6 \times 3 = 18$

you also know that: $\qquad$ $18 \div 6 = 3$

and that: $\qquad$ $18 \div 3 = 6$

In the same way, **doubling** is the **inverse** (opposite) of **halving**.

If you know that: $\qquad$ $2 \times 5 = 10$

you also know that: $\qquad$ $\frac{1}{2}$ of $10 = 5$

and that: $\qquad$ $10 \div 2 = 5$

Exercise 7.6: The inverse

Copy these calculations and complete them by putting the missing number in the box.

1. (a) 7 x 4 = ☐

   (b) 28 ÷ 4 = ☐

   (c) 28 ÷ 7 = ☐

2. (a) 6 x 5 = ☐

   (b) ☐ ÷ 5 = 6

   (c) 30 ÷ ☐ = 5

3. (a) ☐ x 6 = 42

   (b) 42 ÷ ☐ = 6

   (c) ☐ ÷ 6 = 7

4. (a) 2 x 6 = ☐

   (b) $\frac{1}{2}$ of ☐ = 6

5. (a) 20 x $\frac{1}{2}$ = ☐

   (b) 10 x ☐ = 20

6. 8 x ☐ = 24

7. ☐ x 5 = 30

8. 24 ÷ 6 = ☐

9. ☐ ÷ 3 = 9

10. 15 ÷ ☐ = 3

11. ☐ ÷ 9 = 4

12. ☐ x 6 = 12

13. 40 ÷ ☐ = 8

14. 6 x ☐ = 18

15. ☐ ÷ 3 = 7

Checking your answers

You can use the idea of the inverse to check your answers.

Examples:

(i) 34 x 2 = 68

   To check that this is correct, divide 68 by 2

   68 ÷ 2 = 34 so the answer is correct.

(ii) 80 ÷ 5 = 16

   To check that this is correct, multiply 16 by 5

   16 x 5 = 80 so the answer is correct.

Exercise 7.7: Checking your answers

Are these calculations right or wrong?

1. 8 x 2 = 16
2. 3 x 4 = 12
3. 5 x 8 = 45
4. 6 x 5 = 30
5. 7 x 3 = 27

6. 12 ÷ 6 = 2
7. 20 ÷ 4 = 4
8. 15 ÷ 5 = 3
9. 9 ÷ 3 = 3
10. 14 ÷ 2 = 8

11. 12 x 6 = 72
12. 13 x 5 = 65
13. 16 x 4 = 74
14. 26 x 2 = 42
15. 17 x 3 = 31

16. 42 ÷ 3 = 14
17. 58 ÷ 4 = 17
18. 90 ÷ 6 = 15
19. 90 ÷ 5 = 18
20. 74 ÷ 2 = 32

The formal method of division

Extension topic

Like addition, subtraction and multiplication, there is a **formal method** for division. Set out your working as shown in the example below.

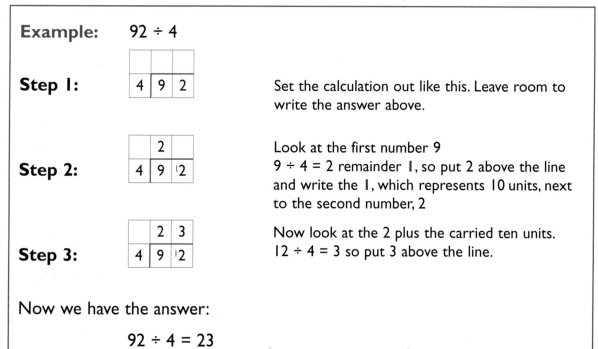

Example: 92 ÷ 4

Step 1:

| 4 | 9 | 2 |

Set the calculation out like this. Leave room to write the answer above.

Step 2:

| | 2 | |
| 4 | 9 | ¹2 |

Look at the first number 9
9 ÷ 4 = 2 remainder 1, so put 2 above the line and write the 1, which represents 10 units, next to the second number, 2

Step 3:

| | 2 | 3 |
| 4 | 9 | ¹2 |

Now look at the 2 plus the carried ten units.
12 ÷ 4 = 3 so put 3 above the line.

Now we have the answer:

92 ÷ 4 = 23

Exercise 7.8: Formal method of division

Extension questions

Calculate, remembering to check your answers (they should be exact):

1. 28 ÷ 2

2. 42 ÷ 3

3. 56 ÷ 4

4. 60 ÷ 5

5. 66 ÷ 6

6. 51 ÷ 3

7. 36 ÷ 2

8. 48 ÷ 4

9. 65 ÷ 5

10. 54 ÷ 2

11. 76 ÷ 2   19. 93 ÷ 3

12. 81 ÷ 3   20. 68 ÷ 4

13. 72 ÷ 4   21. 57 ÷ 3

14. 80 ÷ 5   22. 96 ÷ 4

15. 96 ÷ 6   23. 78 ÷ 6

16. 84 ÷ 3   24. 90 ÷ 2

17. 84 ÷ 2   25. 56 ÷ 4

18. 70 ÷ 5   26. 78 ÷ 6

Rounding: What makes sense?

Sometimes answers will not be exact and have to be rounded up or down to make sense. Look at the next example – you can't hire part of a taxi!

Examples:

(i) A taxi is allowed to carry 4 passengers. How many taxis are needed to take 10 people to the cinema?

10 ÷ 4 = 2 remainder 2

In real life 3 taxis would be needed otherwise 2 people would be left behind, so round **up**.

(ii) Liquorice sticks cost 6 pence each. How many can be bought for 50 pence?

50 ÷ 6 = 8 remainder 2

Only 8 liquorice sticks can be bought, so round **down**.

Problem solving

When solving a problem, whether you are solving it in your head or working on paper, you must write down the calculation you are doing. It also helps to use a few words to explain what the numbers mean.

> **Example:**
>
> 3 friends share a box of 36 chocolates equally among themselves. How many chocolates does each friend get?
>
> Number of chocolates is $36 \div 3 = 12$
>
> Each friend gets 12 chocolates.

Exercise 7.9: Problem solving

1. 2 brothers share 32 biscuits between them. How many biscuits does each brother have?

2. 5 mothers pay £85 to join the Mother & Baby group. How much does it cost each mother to join?

3. Rolls are packed in boxes of 4. How many boxes are needed to pack 60 rolls?

4. A packet of weedkiller is enough to cover 6 square metres of path. How many packets of weedkiller are needed to cover 50 square metres of path?

5. A bowl contains 64 strawberries. Jo eats a quarter of them. How many strawberries does Jo eat?

6. Charlie's scooter uses 3 litres of petrol on every lap of the racing circuit. How many laps can Charlie complete with 48 litres of petrol?

7. Strips of coloured labels cost 10 pence each. How many strips can Colette buy for 58 pence?

8. Sheila earns £75 in 5 days helping out at the beach shop. How much does she earn each day?

9. Tamsin, Diana and Harriet each score the same number of marks in a spelling test. Altogether they get **69** marks. How many marks does each girl get?

10. A bowler completes an over every time he bowls **6** balls. Andrew bowls **78** balls. How many overs has Andrew bowled?

Summary

Make sure you know your 2, 3, 4, 5, 6 and 10 times tables (look back at pages 65-66 to remind yourself if you have forgotten).

> Remember:
>
> - Sometimes an answer will be exact (e.g. 18 ÷ 3 = 6) but sometimes there will be a remainder (e.g. 23 ÷ 5 = 4 remainder 3)
>
> - When **dividing by 10** the digits **move 1 place to the right.**
>
> - When **dividing by 100** the digits **move 2 places to the right.**
>
> - 'A half $(\frac{1}{2})$ of' means 'divide by 2'; 'a quarter $(\frac{1}{4})$ of' means 'divide by 4'; and so on.

Make sure you can use both methods of division.

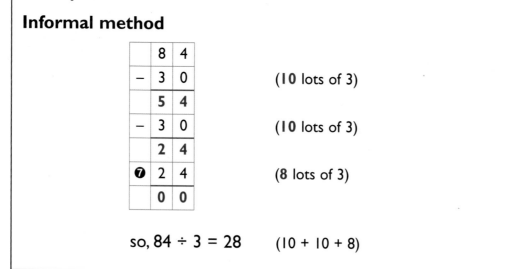

Example: 84 ÷ 3

Informal method

	8	4
−	3	0
	5	4
−	3	0
	2	4
❼	2	4
	0	0

(10 lots of 3)

(10 lots of 3)

(8 lots of 3)

so, 84 ÷ 3 = 28   (10 + 10 + 8)

Formal method (Extension topic)

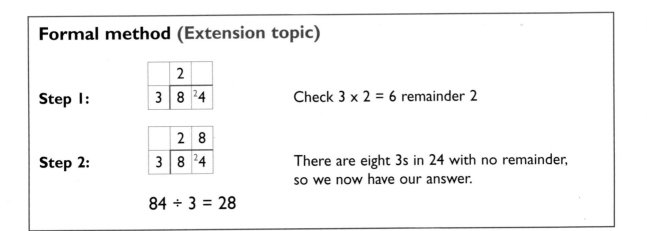

Step 1:

	2	
3	8	²4

Check 3 x 2 = 6 remainder 2

Step 2:

	2	8
3	8	²4

There are eight 3s in 24 with no remainder, so we now have our answer.

$$84 \div 3 = 28$$

Exercise 7.10: Summary exercise

1. Calculate the following, remembering to include any remainder in your answer:

(a) 18 ÷ 2

(b) 30 ÷ 5

(c) 40 ÷ 4

(d) 14 ÷ 3

(e) 18 ÷ 5

(f) 82 ÷ 10

(g) 21 ÷ 3

(h) 35 ÷ 5

(i) 18 ÷ 6

(j) 14 ÷ 2

(k) 16 ÷ 4

(l) 11 ÷ 3

(m) 40 ÷ 5

(n) 11 ÷ 2

(o) 24 ÷ 6

(p) 24 ÷ 4

(q) 24 ÷ 5

(r) 24 ÷ 3

(s) 24 ÷ 10

(t) 24 ÷ 2

2. Calculate the following (all the answers are exact):

(a) 150 ÷ 10   (f) A quarter of 60   (k) 78 ÷ 6

(b) 900 ÷ 100   (g) 54 ÷ 2   (l) 74 ÷ 2

(c) 700 ÷ 10   (h) 78 ÷ 3   (m) 95 ÷ 5

(d) 1200 ÷ 100   (i) 52 ÷ 4   (n) 66 ÷ 3

(e) $\frac{1}{2}$ of 58   (j) 70 ÷ 5   (o) 96 ÷ 6

End of chapter activity: Mixed signs

1. A +, −, x or ÷ sign is missing from each of these statements. Copy out the questions and put in the correct sign, to make the statements true.

(a) (i) 6 ☐ 3 = 18   (b) (i) 10 ☐ 5 = 5   (c) (i) 8 ☐ 4 = 2

(ii) 6 ☐ 3 = 9   (ii) 10 ☐ 5 = 2   (ii) 8 ☐ 4 = 12

(iii) 6 ☐ 3 = 2   (iii) 10 ☐ 5 = 15   (iii) 8 ☐ 4 = 4

(iv) 6 ☐ 3 = 3   (iv) 10 ☐ 5 = 50   (iv) 8 ☐ 4 = 32

2. Copy out the questions and put in the correct number, to make the statements true.

(a) ☐ + 3 = 9   (c) ☐ x 3 = 9

(b) ☐ − 3 = 9   (d) ☐ ÷ 3 = 9

3. Copy out the questions and put in the correct number, to make the statements true.

(a) 15 ÷ ☐ = 5   (c) 15 + ☐ = 30

(b) 15 − ☐ = 5   (d) 15 x ☐ = 30

Did you know?

Numbers cannot be divided by 0 because to divide you have to share a number into groups of a smaller number and you cannot have a group of 0!

Chapter 8: Sequences

A sequence is a series of numbers or a pattern which is formed following a rule. Times tables are sequences: you can find the next multiples of a number by repeatedly adding that number.

Example:

Think back to the 4 times table. To find the next multiple, you add 4 each time: 4   8   12   16

Even and odd numbers

Here is another sequence. All numbers are alternately odd and even.

Odd		Odd		Odd		Odd		Odd	
1	2	3	4	5	6	7	8	9	10
	Even		Even		Even		Even		Even

Odd numbers end in 1, 3, 5, 7 or 9

Even numbers end in 2, 4, 6, 8 or 0 and are multiples of 2

Both even and odd numbers form a sequence where you can find the next term by adding 2

Odd: 1   (+2)   3   (+2)   5   (+2)   7   ...

Even: 2   (+2)   4   (+2)   6   (+2)   8   ...

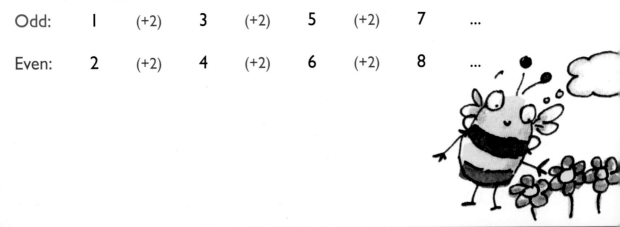

These facts are very helpful.

Fact	Example
Even + even = even	2 + 4 = 6
Even + odd = odd	2 + 1 = 3
Odd + even = odd	5 + 4 = 9
Odd + odd = even	3 + 7 = 10
Even − even = even	8 − 6 = 2
Even − odd = odd	6 − 5 = 1
Odd − even = odd	9 − 2 = 7
Odd − odd = even	7 − 3 = 4
Even x even = even	2 x 4 = 8
Even x odd = even	2 x 3 = 6
Odd x even = even	5 x 2 = 10
Odd x odd = odd	3 x 5 = 15

Continuing sequences

To continue a sequence you must find out what the rule is and apply it.

Examples:

(i) :   :.   :..   :...   Rule: Add 1 •   :....   :.....
                                to the bottom line

(ii) .   ..   .   Rule: Add 1 •   ....
                                to the vertical line
                                and 1 • to the
                                horizontal line

(iii)	2	4	6	8	Rule: Add 2	10	12
(iv)	37	32	27	22	Rule: Subtract 5	17	12
(v)	1	2	4	8	Rule: Multiply by 2	16	32
(vi)	64	32	16	8	Rule: Halve or divide by 2	4	2

Exercise 8.1: Sequences

1. Copy and complete the following sequences and add the next two patterns in each:

   (a)

   (b)

   (c)

   (d)

2. For each of these sequences:

   (i) Write down the next two terms; and (ii) Write down the rule:

   (a) 1   3   5   7   ...   ...
   (b) 10   12   14   16   ...   ...
   (c) 2   5   8   11   ...   ...
   (d) 21   19   17   15   ...   ...
   (e) 56   51   46   41   ...   ...
   (f) 19   16   13   10   ...   ...
   (g) 5   10   15   20   ...   ...

(h) 3   6   9   12   ...   ...

(i) 8   16   24   32   ...   ...

(j) 36   30   24   18   ...   ...

(k) 30   27   24   21   ...   ...

(l) 160   80   40   20   ...   ...

(m) 9   18   27   36   ...   ...

(n) 49   42   35   28   ...   ...

(o) 50   40   30   20   ...   ...

3. Copy and complete these sequences and fill in the missing numbers:

(a) 1   2   3   ...   5   ...

(b) 2   4   ...   8   10   ...

(c) 13   11   ...   7   5   ...

(d) ...   5   9   13   ...   21

(e) 45   40   25

(f) 7   14   21   ...   ...

(g) 25   50   125

(h) 15   ...   45   60   ...

(i) 450   400   350   ...   ...

(j) 200   140   120

End of chapter activity: Test your friends

Make up your own sequences and ask your classmates to solve them.

Make sure you know the correct answers!

Did you know?

No pattern   *Stripes*   *Spots*

Have you ever wondered why the coats of some animals are spotted, others are striped and some have no pattern at all?

Well some very clever mathematicians came up with a calculation that appears to provide an answer.

The mathematical calculation describes a link between the size of an embryo (a cluster of cells in a mummy's tummy that forms into a baby) and when the coat is formed.

If the coat is formed when the embryo is very small the animal will have no pattern (e.g. a mouse), if it is a little bigger a striped pattern is formed, it will have a spotted pattern if it is bigger still and no pattern if it is very big (e.g. an elephant).

Chapter 9: Money

Have you looked closely at the money we use in this country? We have two kinds: paper money (notes) and coins.

There are £50, £20, £10 and £5 notes.

There are £2, £1, 50p, 20p, 10p, 5p, 2p and 1p coins.

Remember: **£1 = 100p**

. . . .

Exercise 9.1: Using coins

1. What is the smallest number of coins you need to make up these sums of money? Write down the coins you use.

   (a) 3 pence   (f) 48 pence

   (b) 7 pence   (g) 66 pence

   (c) 9 pence   (h) 180 pence

   (d) 11 pence   (i) 222 pence

   (e) 25 pence   (j) 599 pence

2. Araminta has one 50p piece, one 20p piece, one 10p piece and one 5p piece.

    Write down all the different sums of money she can make with these four coins using them in groups of one, two, three or four at a time.

3. How many 20 pence pieces make £1?

4. Mr Wilson pays the exact amount of money for his newspaper. He pays with:

    2 x 20 pence coins;

    1 x 10 pence piece;

    2 x 2 pence pieces; and

    1 x 1 penny piece.

    What is the cost of the newspaper?

5. Patricia has 5 coins (all different) which are each worth less than a pound. What is:

    (a) the greatest amount of money she can have?

    (b) the smallest amount of money she can have?

6. 25 pence can be made up with a 20 pence and a 5 pence coin. How can 25 pence be made up with 4 coins?

7. How many 2 pence coins are worth the same as 3 x 10 pence coins?

8. You have two £50 notes, two £20 notes, two £10 notes and two £5 notes. How much money do you have in total?

9. All articles at a market stall cost either 99 pence or 49 pence. Which value of coin must the stall holder have a good supply of, so that he can always give the correct change?

10. A parking meter will take the following coins: 5p, 10p, 20p, 50p, £1. It gives no change. Mr Perkins has a £1 coin, a 50 pence, 3 x 20 pence pieces and a 5 pence. Can Mr Perkins pay the parking charge of £2.25 exactly?

Writing sums of money

You need to learn how to write down sums of money – otherwise you could get into an awful mess! Look closely at the pictures on page 101 and make sure you know what each note or coin is worth.

First let us remember again that £1 = 100 pence.

A **whole number of pounds (£)** can be written in two different ways. For example, seven pounds can be written as:

£7

or **£7.00** (7 pounds and 00 pence)

Tips:

- Can you see the dot between the 7 and 00? This is called the **decimal point** and is used to separate the pounds from the pence.

- When you use a **£ sign**, always use **two figures** for pence (like the 00 above).

- You could write seven pounds as 700p, but this is very unusual.

An amount less than £1 consists only of pence (p) but can still be written in two different ways. For example, fifty-six pence can be written as:

56p

or **£0.56** (0 pounds and 56 pence)

Tips:

- Make sure you know the difference between £0.50 (50 pence) and £0.05 (5 pence).

- Notice that £ and p are **never** used at the same time.

- The £ sign is written **before** the sum of money.

- The p for pence is written **after** the sum of money.

Conversion of pounds to pence

To convert a sum of money from **pounds to pence**, simply **multiply by 100** (the figures move 2 places to the left). Don't forget to use the £ sign or p if you need to.

Examples:	£4 = 400p	£0.95 = 95p
	£12 = 1200p	£0.20 = 20p
	£2.40 = 240p	£0.02 = 2p

Exercise 9.2: Converting pounds to pence

Convert these sums of money to pence:

1. £5
2. £25
3. £175
4. £3.64
5. £9.99

6. £0.37
7. £0.70
8. £0.08
9. £0.10
10. £1.01

11. £0.75
12. £2.43
13. £1.90
14. £0.09
15. £4.42

16. £0.25
17. £9
18. £90
19. £900
20. £99.99

Conversion of pence to pounds

To convert a sum of **money to pounds**, simply **divide by 100** (the figures move 2 places to the right).

Examples:	300p = £3 (£3.00)	75p = £0.75
	1500p = £15 (£15.00)	60p = £0.60
	675p = £6.75	6p = £0.06

Exercise 9.3: Converting pence to pounds

Convert these sums of money to pounds:

1. 200p
2. 150p
3. 240p
4. 148p
5. 995p

6. 370p
7. 307p
8. 38p
9. 9p
10. 90p

11. 86p
12. 375p
13. 1p
14. 205p
15. 250p

16. 25p
17. 5000p
18. 500p
19. 50p
20. 5p

Adding money

If all the sums of money you have been asked to add together are in **pence**, you can set the question out like an **ordinary addition sum**.

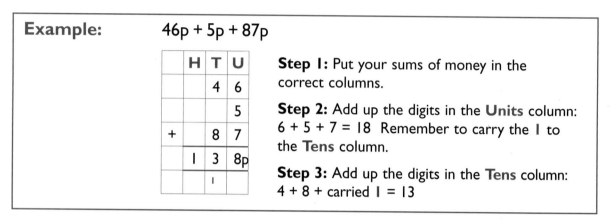

Example: 46p + 5p + 87p

	H	T	U
		4	6
			5
+		8	7
	1	3	8p
		1	

Step 1: Put your sums of money in the correct columns.

Step 2: Add up the digits in the **Units** column: 6 + 5 + 7 = 18 Remember to carry the 1 to the **Tens** column.

Step 3: Add up the digits in the **Tens** column: 4 + 8 + carried 1 = 13

When the answer is more than 100p, write it in pounds. So, in the example above, we calculated that:

46p + 5p + 87p = 138p = £1.38

If all the sums of money are in **pounds**, you need to **line up the decimal points** in the correct columns.

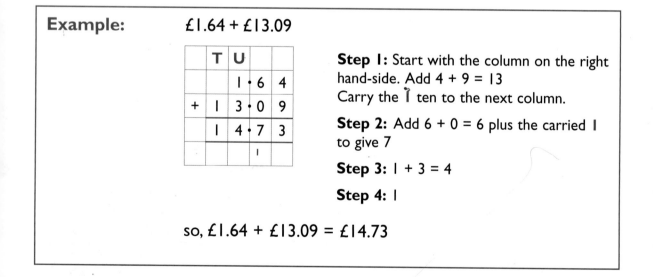

Example: £1.64 + £13.09

	T	U		
		1 · 6	4
+	1	3 · 0	9
	1	4 · 7	3
			1

Step 1: Start with the column on the right hand-side. Add 4 + 9 = 13
Carry the 1 ten to the next column.

Step 2: Add 6 + 0 = 6 plus the carried 1 to give 7

Step 3: 1 + 3 = 4

Step 4: 1

so, £1.64 + £13.09 = £14.73

If there is a **mixture of pounds and pence**, work in **pounds**.

Example: £3.29 + 49p + £11.99

		T	U		
			3 · 2	9	
			0 · 4	9	
+	1	1 · 9	9		
£	1	5 · 7	7		
		1	2		

so, £3.29 + 49p + £11.99 = £15.77

Exercise 9.4: Adding money

1. Calculate:

(a) 37p + 55p

(b) 43p + 29p

(c) 7p + 54p

(d) 83p + 25p

(e) 29p + 6p

(f) 27p + 46p + 18p

(g) 39p + 49p + 99p

(h) 47p + 21p + 5p

(i) 8p + 49p + 57p

(j) 64p + 83p + 95p

2. Calculate:

(a) £3.42 + £1.27

(b) £4.38 + £2.29

(c) £1.95 + £4.05

(d) £1.75 + £2.45

(e) £12.65 + £8.87

(f) £1.23 + £2.12

(g) £3.27 + £4.26

(h) £4.83 + £2.51

(i) £8.65 + £6.17

(j) £4.09 + £16.01

3. Calculate the total of these mixed sums of money (show all your workings):

(a) £1.46 + 43p

(b) £2.39 + 45p

(c) £5.86 + 65p

(d) 89p + £2.55

(e) 7p + £1.16

(f) £1.63 + 49p

(g) £4.67 + 71p

(h) 95p + £2.71

(i) £1.59 + 9p

(j) 38p + £0.29

Subtracting money

Adding on

When subtracting, it is often easier to 'add on'. This means that we start with the lower sum of money and build up to the higher.

Examples:

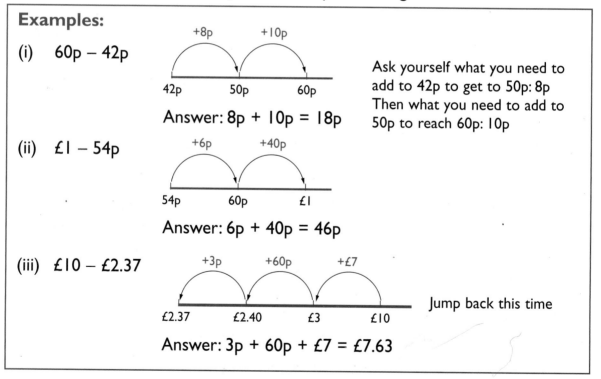

(i) 60p – 42p

+8p   +10p

42p   50p   60p

Answer: 8p + 10p = 18p

Ask yourself what you need to add to 42p to get to 50p: 8p
Then what you need to add to 50p to reach 60p: 10p

(ii) £1 – 54p

+6p   +40p

54p   60p   £1

Answer: 6p + 40p = 46p

(iii) £10 – £2.37

+3p   +60p   +£7

£2.37   £2.40   £3   £10

Jump back this time

Answer: 3p + 60p + £7 = £7.63

Always double-check your answer by adding the sum to be subtracted to your answer. So for Example (iii) above: £7.63 + £2.37 = £10

So, the answer we calculated is correct!

The formal method of subtraction

Extension topic

You can also use the formal method of subtraction that you learnt in Chapter 4 to subtract sums of money.

As with addition, when you subtract one sum of money from another, there are a few things you need to remember.

- When the answer is more than 100p, write it in pounds.

- If all the sums of money are in **pounds**, you need to **line up the decimal points** in the correct columns.

- If there is a **mixture of pounds and pence**, work in **pounds**.

Example:	£12.39 – 99p

	T	**U**		
	1	^{1}2·^{1}3	9
É		0·9	9
£	1	1·4	0

Start on the right-hand side.

Step 1: 9 – 9 = 0

Step 2: Can't subtract 9 from 3 so need to borrow 1 from units column: 13 – 9 = 4

Step 3: 1 – 0 = 1

Step 4: 1

Exercise 9.5: Subtracting money

1. Calculate the following by 'adding on':

(a) 50p – 18p

(b) 80p – 47p

(c) 75p – 39p

(d) £1 – 56p

(e) £2 – 63p

(f) £5 – 86p

(g) £5 – £1.75

(h) £5 – £4.08

(i) £10 – £6.45

(j) £15 – £11.49

Extension questions

2. Calculate the following using the formal method:

(a) 94p – 17p

(b) 75p – 49p

(c) £0.80 – 38p

(d) £9.30 – £7.52

(e) £22.50 – £8.87

(f) £8 – £3.86

(g) £3.55 – 87p

(h) £1.05 – 8p

(i) £10 – 42p

(j) £50 – £17.38

Multiplying money

Always look for ways to work out the answer in your head.

Examples:

(i) 49p x 3 = [50p x 3] – [1p x 3]   Clue: Think of 50 as 49 – 1

= £1.50 – 3p

= £1.47

(ii) 65p x 6 = [60p x 6] + [5p x 6]   Clue: Think of 65 as 60 + 5

= £3.60 + 30p

= £3.90

(iii) £2.70 x 4 = [[£2.70 x 2] x 2   Clue: Think of 4 as 2 x 2

= £5.40 x 2

= £10.80

You will have come across and learnt some of these ideas already.

Exercise 9.6: Multiplying money in your head

Calculate (make notes if you wish - it is useful to show all your workings):

1. 10p x 3
2. 20p x 4
3. 80p x 5
4. 65p x 2
5. 50p x 3

6. 75p x 8
7. 45p x 9
8. 37p x 3
9. 98p x 4
10. 48p x 6

11. 99p x 6
12. £1.50 x 8
13. £1.25 x 5
14. £2.60 x 4
15. £3.50 x 10

16. £7 x 5
17. £6.50 x 2
18. £2.40 x 3
19. £10.40 x 10
20. £5.50 x 8

Problem solving

Make sure you show how you arrive at your answer. Writing things down in words will help you to explain your working.

Example:

In a bakery   Currant buns cost 15p each
                           Muffins cost 18p each

Penny buys 6 currant buns and 4 muffins.

(a)   How much does Penny pay altogether?

        Buns cost 15 x 6 = 90p
        Muffins cost 18 x 4 = 72p
        Total cost is 90p + 72p = £1.62

(b)   How much change should Penny receive if she pays with a £5 note?

        Change is £5 − £1.62 = £3.38

Exercise 9.7: Problem solving

1.   Conrad buys an ice cream for 45 pence and a can of drink for 37 pence. How much money does he spend altogether?

2.   Jenny buys a hair band for 27 pence. How much change should she receive from a 50 pence piece?

3.   What is the cost of three 24 pence stamps?

4.   3 sisters want to have a donkey ride. It costs 75 pence for each girl. How much do the sisters pay in total?

5.   Mr Mallam pays £1.35 to travel by train from Seaville to Paxton. How much change should he get if he pays with a £2 coin?

6.   Mrs Purl buys a knitting pattern and four balls of wool for £5. What is the cost of the pattern if the wool costs £3.85?

7.   A jar of coffee costs £3.20. What is the total cost of 5 jars of coffee?

8.   Gino goes to a pizza restaurant and sees that there is a special offer:

   Pizza £4.75 each or, as a Special Offer, buy 2 for £9

   How much money does Gino save when he buys 2 pizzas at the special price?

9.   A cinema was advertising tickets for sale:

   Alpha Cinema
   Adults   £5.00
   Children   half price

   (a) What is the cost of a child's ticket?

   (b) How much does it cost for 2 adults and 3 children to go to the cinema?

10. An Italian cafe was advertising the price of their sandwiches:

   Sandwich price list
   Egg   90p
   Cheese   95p
   Ham   £1.20
   Tuna   £1.35
   Beef   £1.50

   Sam buys 1 cheese, 1 tuna and 1 beef sandwich:

   (a) What do the sandwiches Sam buys cost altogether?

   Sam pays with a £10 note.

   (b) How much change should he receive?

   Helga buys 1 ham sandwich and 2 egg sandwiches.

   (c) How much does Helga pay for her sandwiches?

   (d) What is the least number of coins Helga can use to pay and what are they?

11. The school shop sells the following items:

Notepad	35p
Pencil	18p
Ballpoint pen	20p
Eraser	22p

    (a) Sue buys a notepad, 3 pencils and an eraser. How much does she spend in total?

    (b) Tom buys 2 notepads and 2 ballpoint pens. How much does he spend?

    (c) Who spends most money, Sue or Tom, and by how much?

12. Tommy opens his piggy bank and finds he has saved 2 x 50p coins, 6 x 20p coins, 13 x 10p coins and 16 x 5p coins.

    (a) How much money has he saved?

    Tommy wants to buy a model car which costs £6.25

    (b) How much more money does he have to save before he can buy the car?

Summary

Conversion

To convert a sum of money **from pounds to pence** you need to **multiply by 100** (figures move 2 places to the left).

Examples:	
	£4 = 400 pence
	£3.45 = 345 pence
	£0.56 = 56 pence
	£0.05 = 5 pence

To convert a sum of money **from pence to pounds** you need to **divide by 100** (figures move 2 places to the right).

Examples	
	500p = £5.00
	385p = £3.85
	34p = £0.34
	8p = £0.08

Addition

Make sure you keep pounds under pounds and pence under pence, in the correct columns.

Example: £12.86 + 75p + £3.69

		T	U		
	1	2 ·	8	6
		0 ·	7	5
+		3 ·	6	9
£	1	7 ·	3	0
		2	2	

Subtraction

You can subtract one sum of money from another by 'adding on'.

Example (i): £3.45 – £1.84   £1.84 → £1.90 → £2.00 → £3.00 → £3.45

| | 6p | 10p | £1.00 | 45p |

Answer: 6p + 10p + £1.00 + 45p = £1.61

Or, you can use the more formal method (**extension topic**).

Example (ii):   £3.45 – £1.84

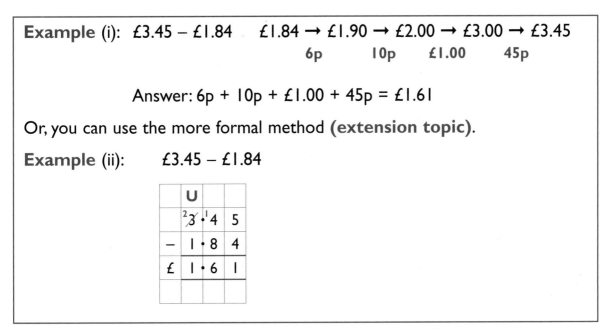

Whichever method you use, always remember to check your answer.

Multiplication

Always look to see whether you can split the numbers up to make the calculations easier.

Example :   £2.65 x 6 = [£2 x 6] + [60p x 6] + [5p x 6]

=   £12   +   £3.60   +   30p

= £15.90

Exercise 9.8: Summary exercise

1. Convert to pence: (a) £2.35   (b) £0.78

2. Write as pounds: (a) 850 pence   (b) 60 pence

3.   Add:

(a) 38p + 75p

(b) £2.48 + £5.17

(c) £1.49 + 68p + £2.27

(d) £1.27 + £2.86 + 7p

(e) £3.85 + £2.63 + £9.95

(f) £27.43 + £5.94 + £35.29

4.   Subtract:

(a) £1 – 37p

(b) £2 – 86p

(c) £6 – £3

(d) £6 – £3.65

(e) £5.50 – £1.63

(f) £4.35 – £2.48

5.   Multiply:

(a) 80p x 2

(b) £1.50 x 3

(c) 75p x 4

(d) £2.50 x 5

(e) £6.25 x 2

(f) £1.43 x 3

End of chapter activity: Shopping

Choose the kind of shop or supermarket department you might like to run: perhaps a sweet shop, paper shop, greengrocer, dairy department or bakery. Do not choose somewhere where the prices are high – no car showrooms!

Visit your choice of shops and write down the price of about 6 items. Draw a picture of each of them, showing the price. Now invite your classmates to shop with you. Make out a bill for what they order and show what the change will be.

Example:	packet of ham	£1.39
	2 packets of butter	£1.24
	6 eggs	£0.48
	Total	£3.11
	Amount paid	£5.00
	Change	£1.89

Did you know?

The highest officially recorded number of children born to one woman is 69. Between 1725 and 1765 the first wife of Feodor Vassilyev (1707-1782) of Shyma, Russia had a total of 27 pregnancies. She gave birth to 16 pairs of twins, seven sets of triplets and four sets of quadruplets.

Can you imagine how much it cost to feed them all? £500 every week

Chapter 10: Introduction to fractions

Think of a pizza. Imagine cutting it in half. Each half is a fraction, a piece of the whole pizza. A **fraction** is a piece of a whole (a unit) where the unit has been divided into equal parts.

A slice of cake is a fraction of the cake.

Recognising a fraction

We write a fraction in a special way.

A fraction is made up of two parts: → $\dfrac{\text{top}}{\text{bottom}}$

The top shows → how many parts we are thinking about
The bottom shows → how many equal parts the whole unit was divided into

The bottom of the fraction gives it its name.

Examples:

(i) Here is a pizza divided into three pieces – thirds. What fraction of the whole pizza does the shaded part represent?

$\dfrac{\text{1 part shaded}}{\text{whole divided into 3 parts}}$ $\dfrac{1}{3}$ one third

One **third** of the pizza is shaded.

(ii) This rectangle is divided into fifths. What fraction of the rectangle is shaded?

$\dfrac{\text{3 parts shaded}}{\text{whole divided into 5 parts}}$ $\dfrac{3}{5}$ three fifths

Three **fifths** of the rectangle is shaded.

Exercise 10.1: Recognising fractions

1. Copy and complete the following (there are lots more to practise on in the Worksheet):

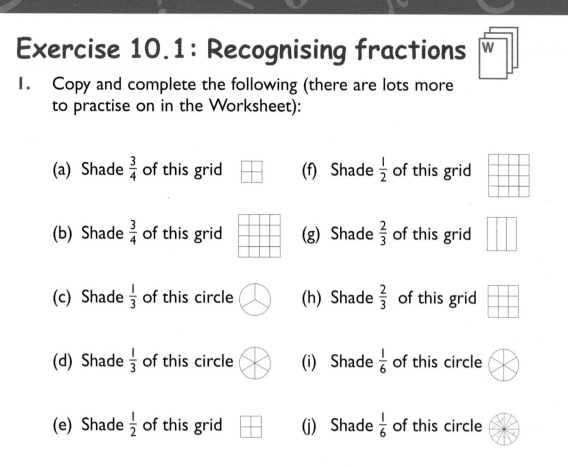

(a) Shade $\frac{3}{4}$ of this grid

(f) Shade $\frac{1}{2}$ of this grid

(b) Shade $\frac{3}{4}$ of this grid

(g) Shade $\frac{2}{3}$ of this grid

(c) Shade $\frac{1}{3}$ of this circle

(h) Shade $\frac{2}{3}$ of this grid

(d) Shade $\frac{1}{3}$ of this circle

(i) Shade $\frac{1}{6}$ of this circle

(e) Shade $\frac{1}{2}$ of this grid

(j) Shade $\frac{1}{6}$ of this circle

2. Write down the fraction of the shape that is: (i) shaded; (ii) unshaded.

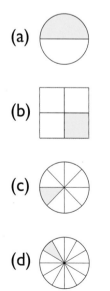

(a)

(e)

(b)

(f)

(c)

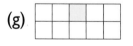

(g)

(d)

(h)

Adding fractions

Look at the shapes in Exercise 10.1 again. In each case, the whole shape is made up of the shaded part and the unshaded part put together. If you add the fraction that represents the shaded part and the fraction that represents the unshaded part together, you will get the whole number 1.

Example:

Shaded part is $\frac{1}{5}$ Unshaded part is $\frac{4}{5}$

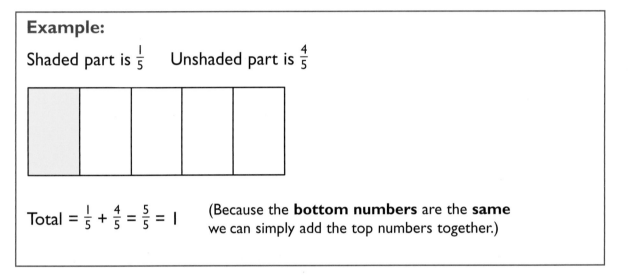

Total $= \frac{1}{5} + \frac{4}{5} = \frac{5}{5} = 1$ (Because the **bottom numbers** are the **same** we can simply add the top numbers together.)

Exercise 10.2: Adding fractions

1. Write down the fraction of the shape that is:
    (i) shaded;   (ii) unshaded.

(a)

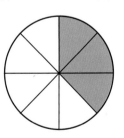

(c)

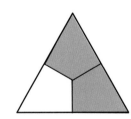

(b)

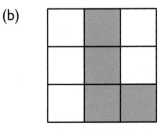

(d)

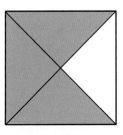

(e)

(h)

(f)

(i)

(g)

(j)

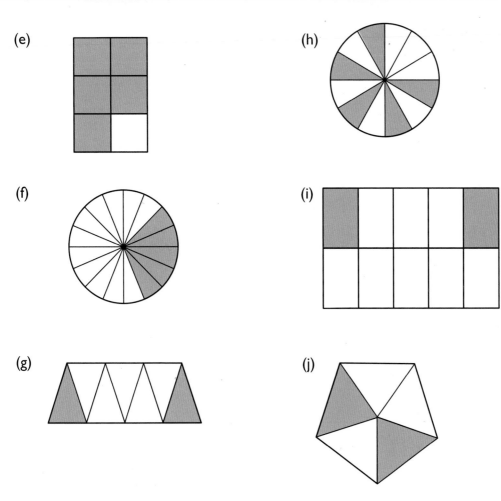

2. Add together your two answers for each part of Q1

3. Copy and complete (there are picture clues to help you):

(a) $\frac{1}{4} + \frac{}{4} = 1$

(f) $\frac{3}{7} + \frac{}{7} = 1$

(b) $\frac{2}{3} + \frac{}{3} = 1$

(g) $\frac{9}{10} + \frac{}{10} = 1$

(c) $\frac{1}{6} + \frac{}{6} = 1$

(h) $\frac{6}{11} + \frac{}{11} = 1$

(d) $\frac{2}{5} + \frac{}{5} = 1$

(i) $\frac{5}{14} + \frac{}{14} = 1$

(e) $\frac{2}{9} + \frac{}{9} = 1$

(j) $\frac{11}{16} + \frac{}{16} = 1$

4. Copy and complete:

(a) $1 - \frac{1}{2} = \frac{}{2}$

(b) $1 - \frac{4}{5} = \frac{}{5}$

(c) $1 - \frac{3}{8} = \frac{}{8}$

(d) $1 - \frac{7}{10} = \frac{}{10}$

(e) $1 - \frac{3}{11} = \frac{}{11}$

(f) $1 - \frac{7}{12} = \frac{}{12}$

(g) $1 - \frac{7}{15} = \frac{}{15}$

(h) $1 - \frac{13}{16} = \frac{}{16}$

(i) $1 - \frac{11}{18} = \frac{}{18}$

(j) $1 - \frac{17}{20} = \frac{}{20}$

Equivalent fractions

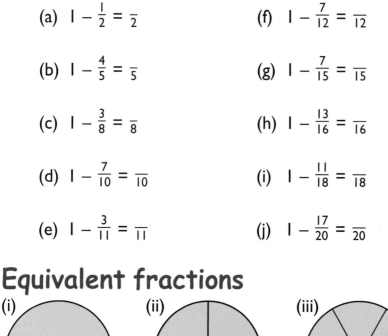

(i) $\frac{1}{2}$ (ii) $\frac{2}{4}$ (iii) $\frac{3}{6}$ (iv) $\frac{4}{8}$

Look closely at the circles above. Each one has been divided into a different number of parts and a different number of the parts have been shaded. For example, in diagram (i) one of the halves has been shaded; in (iii) three of the sixths have been shaded. But do you notice that in each we have in fact shaded half of the circle?

$\frac{1}{2}$ is the **same** size as $\frac{2}{4}$, $\frac{3}{6}$ and $\frac{4}{8}$ The fractions are in fact all the same. We call them **equivalent fractions**. Each of them is a half.

Look at this pizza. It was cut into eight pieces and four have been eaten. We can say that half of the pizza is left or that 4 slices are left. However you describe it, it means the same (equivalent) thing.

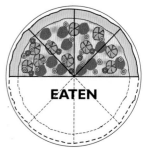

EATEN

The diagram below shows the relationship between different fractions.

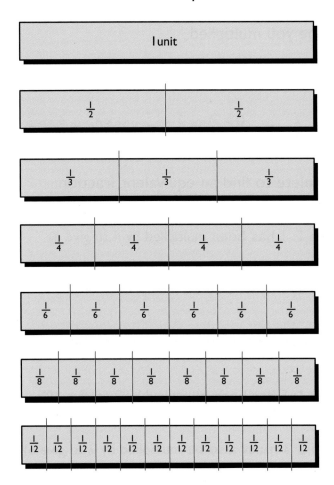

Exercise 10.3: Equivalent fractions (1)

Write down all the fractions you can find that are equivalent to:

1. $\frac{1}{3}$

2. $\frac{1}{4}$

3. $\frac{1}{6}$

4. $\frac{2}{3}$

5. $\frac{3}{4}$

6. $\frac{5}{6}$

We can find equivalent fractions by **multiplying** the **top** and the **bottom** of a fraction by the **same** number. The fraction you end up with will be equivalent to the one you multiplied.

Examples:

(i) $\dfrac{1}{2} = \dfrac{(1 \times 2)}{(2 \times 2)} = \dfrac{2}{4} = \dfrac{(1 \times 3)}{(2 \times 3)} = \dfrac{3}{6} = \dfrac{(1 \times 4)}{(2 \times 4)} = \dfrac{4}{8} = \dfrac{(1 \times 6)}{(2 \times 6)} = \dfrac{6}{12}$

(ii) Copy and complete to find an equivalent fraction:

$\dfrac{1}{3} = \dfrac{4}{}$ (**Step 1: 1 has been** multiplied by 4 to give 4)

$\dfrac{1}{3} = \dfrac{4}{12}$ (**Step 2: 3 must also be** multiplied by 4 to give 12)

(iii) Copy and complete to find an equivalent fraction:

$\dfrac{3}{5} = \dfrac{}{10}$ (**Step 1: 5 has been** multiplied by 2 to give 10)

$\dfrac{3}{5} = \dfrac{6}{10}$ (**Step 2: 3 must also be** multiplied by 2 to give 6)

Exercise 10.4: Equivalent fractions (2)

1. Copy these rectangles into your book and shade half of each one of them.

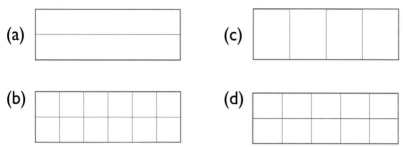

(a)

(c)

(b)

(d)

2. Copy these rectangles into your book and shade one third of each one of them.

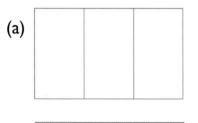

(a)

(c)

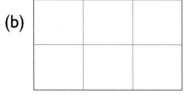

(b)

(d)

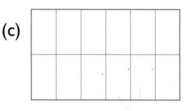

3. What fraction of each rectangle is shaded?

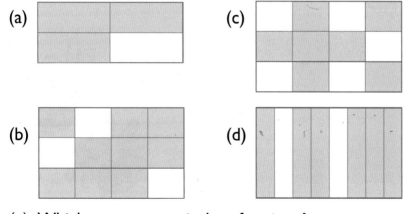

(a)

(c)

(b)

(d)

(e) Which ones are equivalent fractions?

4. Draw four rectangles in your book, each 4 units by 5 units. Shade the following fractions:

(a) $\frac{10}{20}$　　　(b) $\frac{1}{2}$　　　(c) $\frac{16}{20}$　　　(d) $\frac{4}{5}$

5. Draw four rectangles in your book, each 4 units by 5 units. Shade each to show equivalent fractions of one half.

6. Fill in the missing numbers to make these fractions equivalent:

(a) $\frac{1}{3} = \frac{2}{}$

(b) $\frac{1}{2} = \frac{3}{}$

(c) $\frac{3}{4} = \frac{9}{}$

(d) $\frac{5}{6} = \frac{10}{}$

(e) $\frac{2}{3} = \frac{4}{}$

(f) $\frac{1}{3} = \frac{}{12}$

(g) $\frac{2}{3} = \frac{}{15}$

(h) $\frac{3}{4} = \frac{}{20}$

(i) $\frac{2}{5} = \frac{}{10}$

(j) $\frac{7}{9} = \frac{}{18}$

7. Fill in the missing numbers to make these fractions equivalent:

(a) $\frac{2}{5} = \frac{6}{}$

(b) $\frac{1}{4} = \frac{5}{}$

(c) $\frac{3}{4} = \frac{12}{}$

(d) $\frac{3}{10} = \frac{9}{}$

(e) $\frac{7}{12} = \frac{14}{}$

(f) $\frac{4}{9} = \frac{}{27}$

(g) $\frac{5}{6} = \frac{}{30}$

(h) $\frac{7}{10} = \frac{}{40}$

(i) $\frac{4}{15} = \frac{}{30}$

(j) $\frac{3}{20} = \frac{}{40}$

Lowest terms

If you divide a pizza into 8 equal pieces and eat 4 of them you don't say you have eaten $\frac{4}{8}$ of the pizza – you say you have eaten $\frac{1}{2}$ of it. You give your answer in its **lowest terms**.

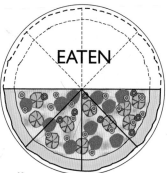

A fraction is in its lowest terms when it cannot be written as an equivalent fraction with fewer parts (or smaller numbers). That is, the top and bottom cannot be divided exactly by the same number (except 1).

Examples:

(i) $\frac{6}{12} = \frac{1}{2}$ in its lowest terms

(ii) $\frac{70}{100} = \frac{7}{10}$ in its lowest terms

To write a fraction in its lowest terms we **divide** the **top** and **bottom** of the fraction by the **same** number.

Examples:

Fill in the missing number to give these fractions in their lowest terms:

(i) $\frac{6}{15} = \frac{2}{}$

                    (6 **has been** divided by 3 to give 2)
                    (15 **must be** divided by 3 to give 5)

     $\frac{6}{15} = \frac{2}{5}$

(ii) $\frac{10}{12} = \frac{}{6}$

                    (12 **has been** divided by 2 to give 6)
                    (10 **must be** divided by 2 to give 5)

     $\frac{10}{12} = \frac{5}{6}$

When working with fractions, make sure your answer is in its lowest terms. Don't worry if you do not get the fraction into its lowest terms in one, or even two, goes – you may have to divide more than once.

Example: Write $\frac{12}{18}$ in its lowest terms.

We can do this in one stage by dividing by the largest factor of both numbers.

$\frac{12}{18} = \frac{2}{3}$ (Top and bottom have been divided by the largest factor, which is 6)

If we can't see what the largest factor is, we can divide by several smaller numbers instead.

$\frac{12}{18} = \frac{6}{9} = \frac{2}{3}$ (Top and bottom have been divided by 2 and then by 3
The result is the same because 2 x 3 = 6)

Always look for the largest factor, so that you can find the fraction's lowest terms in just one step.

Tips:

- 2 is a factor of all even numbers
- 5 is a factor of all numbers ending in 5 or 0
- Watch out for multiples of 3

Exercise 10.5: Lowest terms

Fill in the missing numbers to make these fractions equivalent in their lowest terms:

1. $\frac{4}{8} = \frac{1}{\underline{}}$

2. $\frac{8}{12} = \frac{4}{\underline{}}$

3. $\frac{8}{10} = \frac{4}{\underline{}}$

4. $\frac{3}{6} = \frac{1}{\underline{}}$

5. $\frac{6}{8} = \frac{3}{\underline{}}$

6. $\frac{6}{18} = \frac{1}{\underline{}}$

7. $\frac{9}{24} = \frac{3}{-}$

14. $\frac{15}{20} = \frac{}{4}$

8. $\frac{10}{15} = \frac{2}{-}$

15. $\frac{25}{35} = \frac{}{7}$

9. $\frac{12}{18} = \frac{2}{-}$

16. $\frac{10}{18} = \frac{}{9}$

10. $\frac{24}{30} = \frac{4}{-}$

17. $\frac{18}{24} = \frac{}{4}$

11. $\frac{4}{12} = \frac{}{3}$

18. $\frac{28}{36} = \frac{}{9}$

12. $\frac{2}{8} = \frac{}{4}$

19. $\frac{18}{30} = \frac{}{5}$

13. $\frac{10}{12} = \frac{}{6}$

20. $\frac{15}{45} = \frac{}{3}$

· ·

Fractions of a number

One part of a fraction

If you want $\frac{1}{2}$ an orange you **divide** the orange into 2 parts.

If you want a $\frac{1}{4}$ of a bar of chocolate you **divide** the bar into 4 parts.

When you want a fraction of a number you **divide** the number by the **denominator** (bottom number) of the fraction.

Example: What is $\frac{1}{3}$ (a third) of 18?

Think of the 18 as a whole (it might help to imagine an 18-segment orange or an 18-piece bar of chocolate!) We need to divide the whole by 3

18 ÷ 3 = 6

$\frac{1}{3}$ of 18 is 6

Exercise 10.6: Fractions of a number (1)

Calculate:

1. $\frac{1}{2}$ of 8

2. $\frac{1}{3}$ of 6

3. $\frac{1}{4}$ of 12

4. $\frac{1}{5}$ of 10

5. $\frac{1}{6}$ of 18

6. $\frac{1}{10}$ of 20

7. $\frac{1}{5}$ of 25

8. $\frac{1}{3}$ of 15

9. $\frac{1}{4}$ of 24

10. $\frac{1}{10}$ of 50

11. $\frac{1}{2}$ of 14

12. $\frac{1}{6}$ of 30

More than one part of a fraction

When you want more than 1 part, start by finding the size of 1 part and then multiply it by the number of parts needed.

Example:	What is $\frac{3}{4}$ (three quarters) of 20?
1 part is:	20 ÷ 4 = 5
3 parts are:	5 x 3 = 15
So $\frac{3}{4}$ of 20 is 15	

Exercise 10.7: Fractions of a number (2)

Calculate:

1. $\frac{2}{3}$ of 15

2. $\frac{2}{5}$ of 15

3. $\frac{3}{10}$ of 50

4. $\frac{3}{5}$ of 20

5. $\frac{3}{4}$ of 24

6. $\frac{9}{10}$ of 30

7. $\frac{5}{6}$ of 12

8. $\frac{4}{5}$ of 25

9. $\frac{7}{10}$ of 40

10. $\frac{3}{4}$ of 40

Summary

1. A fraction is part of a whole.

The top shows $\rightarrow$
The bottom shows $\rightarrow$

$$\frac{\text{number of equal parts selected}}{\text{total number of equal parts the unit has been divided into}}$$

In this picture $\frac{5}{8}$ is shaded

and $\frac{3}{8}$ is unshaded

$\frac{5}{8} + \frac{3}{8} = \frac{8}{8} = 1$

Note: When the top number is 1, the **smaller** the bottom number, the **larger** the fraction.

Example:	$\frac{1}{2}$ is larger than $\frac{1}{4}$

2. **Equivalent fractions** are **equal**.

   The top **and** the bottom are **both** either **multiplied** or **divided** by the same number.

   $\frac{3}{4} = \frac{9}{12}$ (Both 3 and 4 have been **multiplied** by 3)

   $\frac{12}{16} = \frac{6}{8}$ (Both 12 and 16 have been **divided** by 2)

3. A fraction is in its **lowest terms** when the **only** number the top and bottom can both be divided by is **1**

Examples:

(i) $\frac{3}{5}$ is in its lowest terms: only 1 goes into both 3 and 5

(ii) $\frac{10}{15}$ can be turned into its lowest terms by dividing top and bottom by 5 to become $\frac{2}{3}$

---

4. To find a **fraction of a quantity**, you must divide by the bottom number and multiply by the top number.

Example: What is $\frac{3}{5}$ (three fifths) of 30?

                       $30 \div 5 = 6$

                       $6 \times 3 = 18$

                       $\frac{3}{5}$ of 30 = 18

Exercise 10.8: Summary exercise

1. Copy and shade $\frac{5}{9}$ of this shape:

2. Draw three copies of a square with sides of 3 centimetres.

   (a) Shade $\frac{7}{9}$ of the square.   (c) Shade $\frac{1}{3}$ of the square.

   (b) Shade $\frac{2}{3}$ of the square.

3. Copy and complete:

   (a) $\frac{11}{16} + \frac{}{16} = 1$ (d) $\frac{5}{12} + \frac{}{12} = 1$

   (b) $\frac{4}{9} + \frac{}{9} = 1$ (e) $\frac{3}{8} + \frac{}{8} = 1$

   (c) $\frac{7}{10} + \frac{}{10} = 1$ (f) $\frac{2}{15} + \frac{}{15} = 1$

4. Charlie has drunk $\frac{7}{12}$ of a bottle of juice. What fraction of juice remains?

5. Which is the larger fraction:

   (a) $\frac{1}{3}$ or $\frac{1}{8}$ (d) $\frac{1}{5}$ or $\frac{1}{6}$

   (b) $\frac{1}{2}$ or $\frac{1}{10}$ (e) $\frac{1}{12}$ or $\frac{1}{16}$

   (c) $\frac{1}{4}$ or $\frac{1}{3}$ (f) $\frac{1}{100}$ or $\frac{1}{10}$

6. Fill in the missing number to make these fractions equivalent:

(a) $\frac{2}{3} = \frac{8}{}$

(c) $\frac{25}{40} = \frac{5}{}$

(b) $\frac{3}{5} = \frac{}{15}$

(d) $\frac{18}{30} = \frac{}{5}$

7. Write these fractions in their lowest terms:

(a) $\frac{15}{18}$

(c) $\frac{10}{15}$

(e) $\frac{8}{18}$

(b) $\frac{12}{16}$

(d) $\frac{20}{30}$

(f) $\frac{12}{21}$

8. Calculate:

(a) $\frac{3}{4}$ of 20

(c) $\frac{2}{5}$ of 20

(e) $\frac{7}{10}$ of 30

(b) $\frac{2}{3}$ of 24

(d) $\frac{5}{6}$ of 12

(f) $\frac{3}{5}$ of 50

. . . .

End of chapter activity: Fractional dominoes

Preparation

Cut out the set of dominoes from the worksheet. (It might be a good idea to stick them onto card to make them easier to handle.)

How to play

Once you have cut out your dominoes you are ready to play. The game is for two players.

● Lay all the dominoes face down on the table.

● Each player picks four cards. The rest remain face down on the table.

- The player with the largest bottom number goes first by placing one of his/her dominoes on the table, face up.

- The next player plays a domino with a matching fraction. Dominoes can be placed only at either end of the line of dominoes in play. If a player does not have a domino with a matching fraction, he/she must forfeit his/her turn and take another card from those still face down on the table.

- Play continues until one of the players has no dominoes left and calls out 'domino!'

The aim is to match fractions as below:

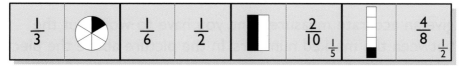

If you get stuck your teacher will be able to explain in more detail how to play the game.

Did you know?

One quarter of the bones in your body are in your feet!

The Himalayas cover one-tenth of the Earth's land surface area!

Chapter 11: Scales, estimation and rounding

If you want to measure the length of a line you will probably use a ruler or tape measure. Have a look at a ruler – can you see that it has numbers on it at regular intervals? It is easy to measure something that is exactly 4 cm long but what happens if the length of something you measure falls between, say, 6 and 7 cm?

In order to give an accurate measurement, you have to work out the numbers in between the marked numbers. In the picture above the piece of string measures six and a half centimetres.

There will be many occasions in which you will need to read scales – when you measure things in maths or science, for example, or when you display data you have collected.

Reading scales

The very first thing we must **always** to do is work out what **one** division (mark) means. Once you have worked this out it is often helpful to write the correct values under each division before reading off the scale .

Examples:

What numbers are the arrows pointing at?

(i)

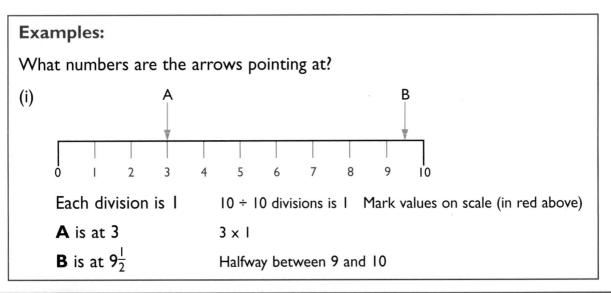

Each division is 1 10 ÷ 10 divisions is 1 Mark values on scale (in red above)

A is at 3   3 x 1

B is at $9\frac{1}{2}$ Halfway between 9 and 10

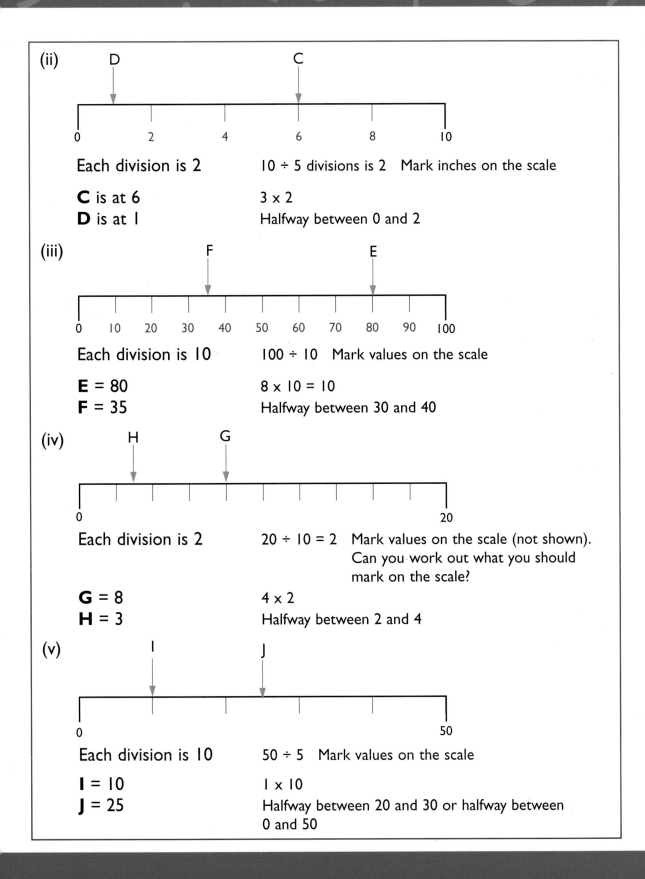

(ii)

Each division is 2   10 ÷ 5 divisions is 2   Mark inches on the scale

C is at 6   3 x 2
D is at 1   Halfway between 0 and 2

(iii)

Each division is 10   100 ÷ 10   Mark values on the scale

E = 80   8 x 10 = 10
F = 35   Halfway between 30 and 40

(iv)

Each division is 2   20 ÷ 10 = 2   Mark values on the scale (not shown).
                            Can you work out what you should
                            mark on the scale?

G = 8   4 x 2
H = 3   Halfway between 2 and 4

(v)

Each division is 10   50 ÷ 5   Mark values on the scale

I = 10   1 x 10
J = 25   Halfway between 20 and 30 or halfway between
                            0 and 50

Exercise 11.1: Reading scales

Write down the numbers that the arrows A, B and C are pointing at:

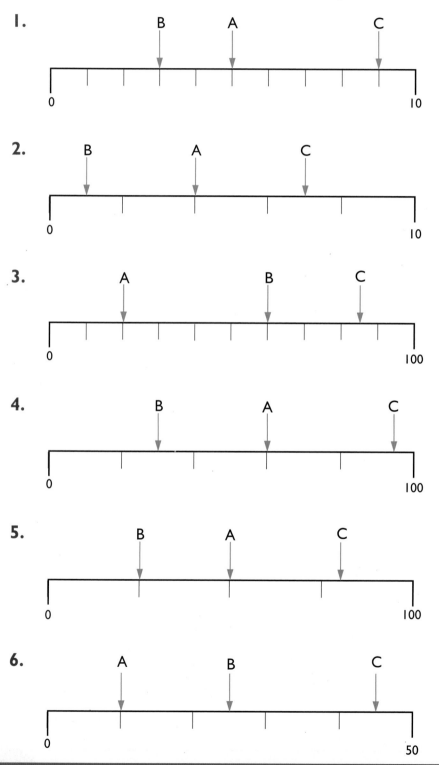

1.

2.

3.

4.

5.

6.

7.

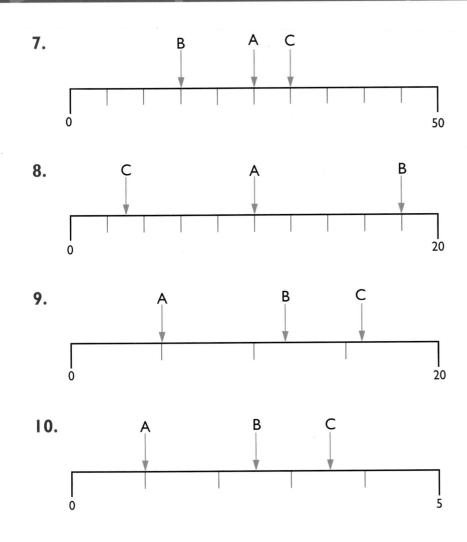

B   A   C

0   50

8.

C   A   B

0   20

9.

A   B   C

0   20

10.

A   B   C

0   5

Marking numbers on a scale

When trying to mark a number on a scale it is useful to work out the halfway mark and then halve the halves to find where the quarter marks are. If it is an accurate scale, using a ruler can also be helpful.

Examples:

Mark the numbers **A**, **B** and **C** with arrows on the number lines below:

(i) **A** = 75, **B** = 40 and **C** = 10

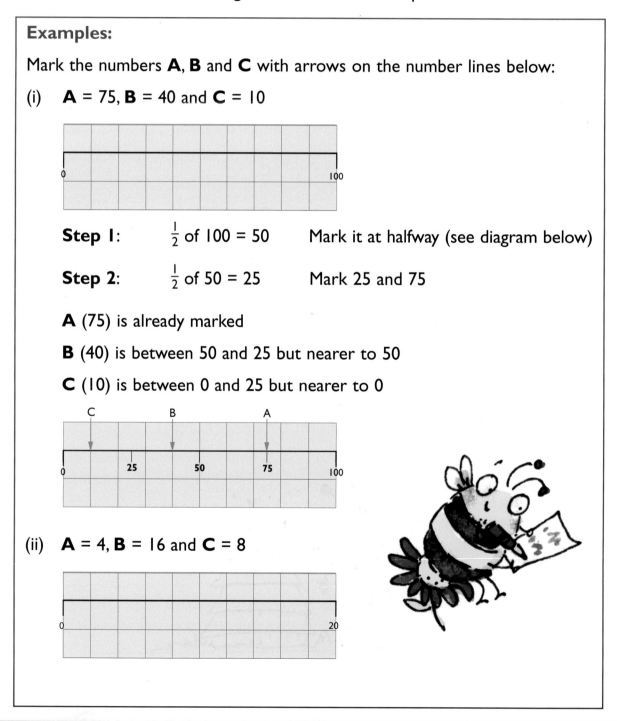

Step 1: $\frac{1}{2}$ of 100 = 50 Mark it at halfway (see diagram below)

Step 2: $\frac{1}{2}$ of 50 = 25 Mark 25 and 75

A (75) is already marked

B (40) is between 50 and 25 but nearer to 50

C (10) is between 0 and 25 but nearer to 0

(ii) **A** = 4, **B** = 16 and **C** = 8

Step 1: $\frac{1}{2}$ of 20 = 10   Mark it at halfway (see diagram below)

Step 2: $\frac{1}{2}$ of 10 = 5   Mark 5 and 15

A (4) is 1 less than 5

B (16) is 1 more than 15

C (8) is between 5 and 10 but nearer to 10

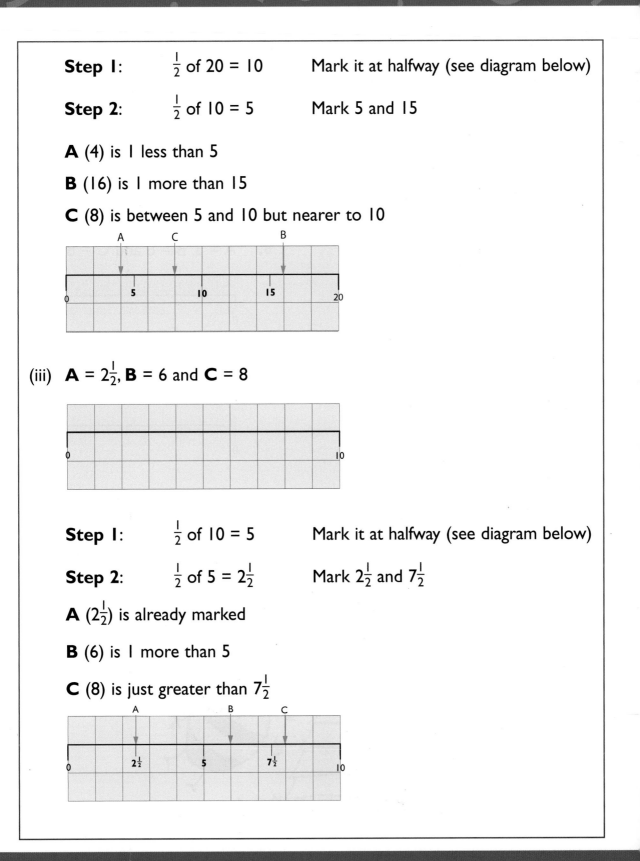

(iii) **A** = $2\frac{1}{2}$, **B** = 6 and **C** = 8

Step 1: $\frac{1}{2}$ of 10 = 5   Mark it at halfway (see diagram below)

Step 2: $\frac{1}{2}$ of 5 = $2\frac{1}{2}$ Mark $2\frac{1}{2}$ and $7\frac{1}{2}$

A ($2\frac{1}{2}$) is already marked

B (6) is 1 more than 5

C (8) is just greater than $7\frac{1}{2}$

Exercise 11.2: Marking numbers on a scale

Copy the scales below and mark the numbers A, B and C with arrows:

1.   A = 50, B = 75 and C = 30

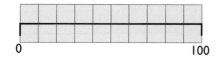

0   100

5.   A = 25, B = 35 and C = 10

0   50

2.   A = 20, B = 40 and C = 65

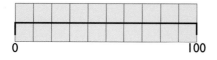

0   100

6.   A = 3, B = 6 and C = 8

0   10

3.   A = 70, B = 45 and C = 90

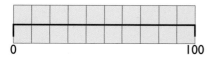

0   100

7.   A = $\frac{1}{2}$, B = $\frac{1}{4}$ and C = $\frac{3}{4}$

0   1

4.   A = 15, B = 30 and C = 45

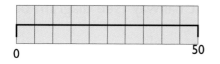

0   50

8.   A = 2, B = 4 and C = $\frac{1}{2}$

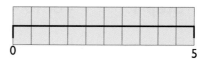

0   5

Rounding numbers

Sometimes the numbers we use do not have to be exact. For example, we might say:

- 'There are about 30 chocolates in a box' (rather than 'there are exactly 32 chocolates').
- 'There were around 100 guests at the party (rather than 'there were exactly 97 guests').

In each case the numbers have been **rounded** to a certain **degree of accuracy**.

Rounding to the nearest ten

When you round a number to the nearest 10, you have decide which multiple of 10 (10, 20, 30, 40, ...) the number is closest to.

Example:

Write each of these numbers to the nearest 10:   (a) 13   (b) 17   (c) 15

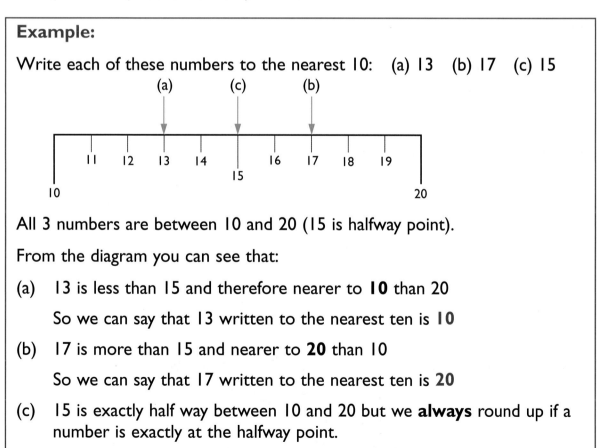

All 3 numbers are between 10 and 20 (15 is halfway point).

From the diagram you can see that:

(a)   13 is less than 15 and therefore nearer to **10** than 20

So we can say that 13 written to the nearest ten is **10**

(b)   17 is more than 15 and nearer to **20** than 10

So we can say that 17 written to the nearest ten is **20**

(c)   15 is exactly half way between 10 and 20 but we **always** round up if a number is exactly at the halfway point.

15 written to the nearest ten is **20**

> **Tip:**
> - If a number falls **below the halfway mark** it is **rounded down**.
> - If a number is **at or above the halfway mark** it is **rounded up**.

Exercise 11.3: Rounding to the nearest ten

1. Write these numbers to the nearest 10:

   (a) 29   (b) 41   (c) 5   (d) 72   (e) 86

2 There are 17 pupils in class 3. How many pupils are there to the nearest 10?

3. There are 62 members of staff. How many staff are there to the nearest 10?

4. The best seat at the theatre costs £85. Write this price to the nearest £10.

5. It is 59 miles from London to Cambridge. What is this distance written to the nearest 10 miles?

6. The school football team scored 34 goals last season. What is this total to the nearest 10?

7. Tanya has mass 45 kilograms. What is her mass to the nearest 10 kilograms?

8. Mr Simpson is driving his car at 61 mph. Write this speed to the nearest 10 mph.

9. Jacques ran the 200 metres in 36 seconds. Write this time to the nearest 10 seconds.

10. A magazine costs 70 pence to the nearest 10 pence. What is the most expensive price it could be?

Rounding to the nearest hundred

When you round a number to the nearest 100, you have decide which multiple of 100 (100, 200, 300, 400, ...) the number is closest to.

Example:

Write each of these numbers to the nearest 100:
    (a) 330   (b) 385   (c) 352

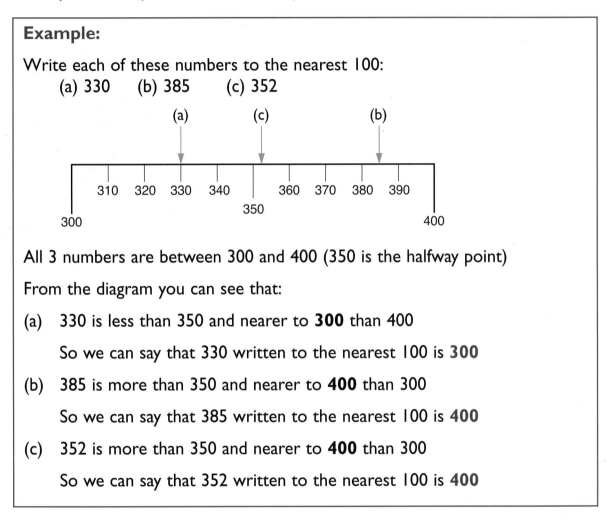

All 3 numbers are between 300 and 400 (350 is the halfway point)

From the diagram you can see that:

(a)   330 is less than 350 and nearer to **300** than 400

     So we can say that 330 written to the nearest 100 is **300**

(b)   385 is more than 350 and nearer to **400** than 300

     So we can say that 385 written to the nearest 100 is **400**

(c)   352 is more than 350 and nearer to **400** than 300

     So we can say that 352 written to the nearest 100 is **400**

Exercise 11.4: Rounding to the nearest hundred

1.   Write these numbers to the nearest 100:

    (a) 729   (b) 643   (c) 296   (d) 187   (e) 450

2.   There are 187 pupils on the school roll. How many pupils are there to the nearest 100?

3.   There are 214 cars in a multi-storey car park. How many cars are there to the nearest 100?

4. A bicycle costs £335. How much does it cost to the nearest £100?

5. Dick Turpin rode 211 miles from London to York. How far did he ride to the nearest 100 miles?

6. The Snipers shooting team scored 750 points. What was their score to the nearest 100?

7. 856 people watched Dribblers United's last match. Write this number to the nearest 100.

8. The postman delivered 149 letters on Tuesday. How many letters was this to the nearest 100?

9. The Zoo Park has an area of 503 hectares. How many hectares is this to the nearest 100?

10. The school library contains 700 books to the nearest hundred. What is the smallest number of books there could be?

Summary

When **reading off** numbers, work out what each division means.

When **marking numbers** on a scale, start by dividing up the line into halves and quarters.

When **rounding**, find the number that is halfway so that you can decide whether to round **up** or **down**. Remember that if a number is exactly halfway you round up.

Exercise 11.5: Summary exercise

1. Write down the numbers shown by the arrows:

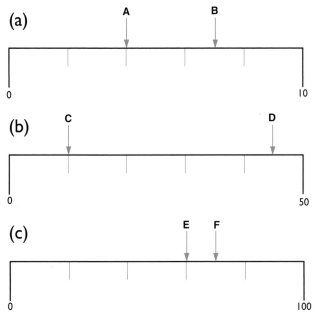

(a)

A   B

0   10

(b)

C   D

0   50

(c)

E   F

0   100

2. Copy the scales below and mark the numbers A and B with arrows:

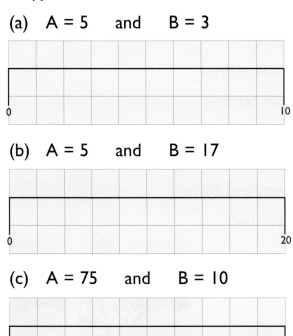

(a) A = 5   and   B = 3

0   10

(b) A = 5   and   B = 17

0   20

(c) A = 75   and   B = 10

0   100

3. Write:

   (a) 76 to the nearest 10

   (b) 15 to the nearest 10

   (c) 23 to the nearest 10

   (d) 87 to the nearest 10

   (e) 91 to the nearest 10

   (f) 85 to the nearest 10

   (g) 84 to the nearest 10

   (h) 52 to the nearest 10

4. Write:

   (a) 234 to the nearest 100

   (b) 195 to the nearest 100

   (c) 403 to the nearest 100

   (d) 375 to the nearest 100

   (e) 384 to the nearest 100

   (f) 209 to the nearest 100

   (g) 290 to the nearest 100

   (h) 195 to the nearest 100

End of chapter activity: Rounding numbers

Write a list of the different types of groups in your school and write down how many people there are in each. For example, you might find out:

- the numbers of pupils in each form;
- the number of pupils in the whole school;
- the number of boys in the whole school;
- the number of girls in the whole school;
- the number of staff;
- the number of pupils in the choir; and so on.

Now write each of these numbers to the nearest 10 or 100

Did you know?

We are about 1 cm taller in the morning than in the evening. Layers of cartilage in the joints gets compressed during the day!

Chapter 12: Measurement – length

In this chapter we are going to look at how we measure things to see how long they are – their **length**. There are various units of measurement, which you will almost certainly have come across in your daily lives:

● A seed you may have measured in science might have been 3 millimetres long.

● Your feet may be 15 centimetres long.

● You may be 1.5 metres tall.

● You may travel 10 kilometres to school.

Units of length

Remember:

● **10 millimetres (mm) = 1 centimetre (cm)**
● **100 centimetres (cm) = 1 metre (m)**
● **1000 metres (m) = 1 kilometre (km)**

Look at a ruler to see the length of a millimetre and a centimetre. Look at the length of a metre on a metre rule.

To measure longer distances you will need a tape measure. Look at it to see what unit of measurement its divisions are in and the greatest distance you could measure with it.

For even longer distances you will need something like a trundle wheel or pedometer. Work out how many steps you have to take to travel a **kilometre**.

Writing measurements

Let us have a look at how we record lengths that are **less than 1 metre** (100 centimetres). We will round them to the nearest $\frac{1}{2}$ (0.5) centimetre.

> **Tip:** Always remember to start measuring at 0!

Example:

Measure and write down the lengths of:
(a) AB   (b) AC   (c) AD   (d) AE

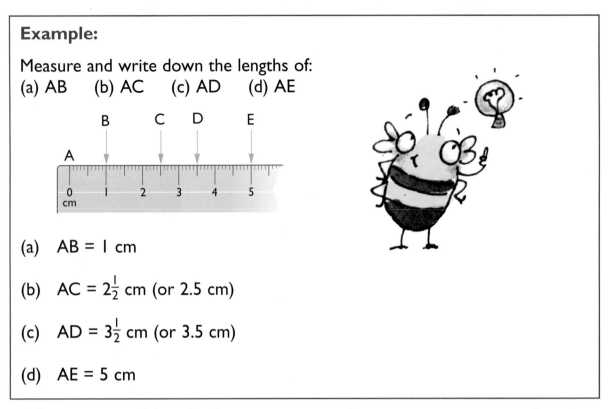

(a)   AB = 1 cm

(b)   AC = $2\frac{1}{2}$ cm (or 2.5 cm)

(c)   AD = $3\frac{1}{2}$ cm (or 3.5 cm)

(d)   AE = 5 cm

When we record lengths that are **greater than a metre** we write them in the same way as we write sums of money that are greater than £.

100 pence = £1   100 centimetres = 1 metre

Examples:

(i)   200p = £2.00   200 cm = 2.00 m

(ii)   230p = £2.30   230 cm = 2.30 m

(iii) 203p = £2.03   203 cm = 2.03 m

It is helpful to remember some fractions of a metre. For example:

● $\frac{1}{2}$ m = 50 cm

● $2\frac{1}{2}$ m = 250 cm

● $2\frac{1}{4}$ m = 225 cm

● $2\frac{3}{4}$ m = 275 cm

Exercise 12.1: Using measurements

1. Write in metres:

   (a) 500 cm

   (b) 165 cm

   (c) 450 cm

   (d) 75 cm

   (e) 189 cm

   (f) 605 cm

   (g) 65 cm

2. Write in centimetres:

   (a) 3 m

   (b) 2.45 m

   (c) $1\frac{1}{4}$ m

   (d) 0.08 cm

   (e) $3\frac{1}{2}$ m

   (f) 1.8 m

   (g) $7\frac{3}{4}$ m

3. John lays 2 pieces of wood, which measure 82 centimetres and 68 centimetres, end to end. What is the length of the 2 pieces of wood altogether?
   Give your answer in (a) centimetres; and (b) metres.

4. Miss Maxwell cuts 3 metres of ribbon into 4 equal pieces. What is the length of each piece? (Hint: work in centimetres.)

5. Gillian jumps 3.72 metres in the long jump. Jo jumps 29 centimetres less than Gillian. How far does Jo jump?

6. A circular coin is 2 centimetres wide.
   (a) How long is a straight line of 80 coins if they touch each other?

   Another line of these coins is 96 centimetres long.
   (b) How many coins are there in this line?

7. 3 runners take part in a relay race which is 400 metres long. Peter runs the first 100 metres and Quentin runs the next 75 metres. Richard runs the rest of the distance. How far does Richard run?

8. A beanstalk grows at the rate of 5 centimetres every day. After how many days will the beanstalk be a metre tall?

9. A snail racing track is half a metre long. Sammy has crawled 27 centimetres along the track from the start. How far is Sammy from the finish?

10. Zia uses 65 centimetres of ribbon to make a Christmas bow. How many metres of ribbon will Zia use to make 10 bows?

Estimating length and practical measurement

When we measure an item, it is useful to make an estimate first. When estimating, look at the item and try to decide whether it is shorter or longer than something you know the length of.

For example, if you are estimating the length of a pencil, it is probably about half the length of a 30 centimetre ruler. If you think it is about $\frac{1}{2}$ as long as a ruler, then you can estimate the length as about 15 cm. If you are measuring the height of a room, and you know how tall you are, you can think about how many times you would have to stand on your own head to reach the ceiling, and use that to help you make an estimate!

Exercise 12.2: Estimating and measuring length

1. Go around the classroom and find items that you can measure. Give 2 answers for each item:

   (a) **Estimate** the length

   (b) **Measure** the length

Example:

Object	Estimate	Measurement
Pencil	12 cm	15.5 cm
Height of door	2 m	1.80 m
Distance to pavilion	150 m	178 m

If your answer is in centimetres, give its measurement to the nearest 0.5 cm. For items that measure more than a metre, give your answer as accurately as your measuring instrument will allow.

End of chapter activity: Make a collection and investigate Imperial units of length

1. (a) Make a collection of labels, packets, boxes, advertisements, cotton reels etc. that refer to length. Rummage around at home and get your family to help you! (Later this could form part of a class presentation on measurement.)

    (b) Record the lengths of your objects and rank them in order of length (smallest first).

2. Millimetres, centimetres and kilometres are the measurements of length we use today. They are part of what is called the **metric system**. Not so long ago we used **Imperial units**. You have probably heard of the measurements inch, foot, yard as well as the mile which we still use today. Find out what you can about them and make a table to show how they compare in length with the metric units.

Did you know?

A giraffe can clean its ears with its 21-inch tongue!

Chapter 13: Measurement – mass

In the last chapter we looked at measuring length; now we are going to investigate the measurement of mass – that is, how heavy things are.

You will probably have measured how heavy something is, its **mass**, on many occasions. For example:

- Weighing ingredients when baking cakes.

- Seeing how much you weigh on the bathroom scales.

Units of mass

Remember:

- 1000 grams (g) = 1 kilogram (kg)

- $\frac{1}{2}$ kg = 500 g

- $\frac{1}{4}$ kg = 250 g

- $\frac{3}{4}$ kg = 750 g

Reading and marking scales

There are various instruments you can use to measure mass. Here are some you may have come across:

We read and mark scales that show mass in the same way as the scales we met in Chapter 11.

● When reading a scale, work out what each small division represents first.

● When marking a scale, work out what half a division, and a quarter of a division, represents.

Exercise 13.1: Reading and marking scales

1. (a) How many grams does each small line represent?

   (b) What mass is arrow A pointing to?

   (c) What mass is arrow B pointing to?

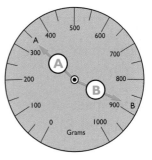

2. (a) How many grams does each small line represent?

   (b) What mass does arrow A show?

   (c) What mass does arrow B show?

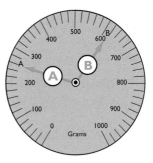

3. (a) How many grams does each small line represent?

   (b) What mass does arrow A show?

   (c) What mass does arrow B show?

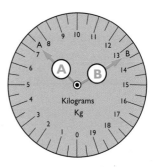

4. Mrs Grumble buys a 225 gram packet of butter and a 670 gram piece of cheese. Copy the dial and mark on it:

    (a) the mass of the butter (use an arrow marked A);

    (b) the mass of the cheese (use an arrow marked B).

    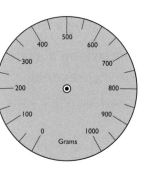

5. Marie went to a post office to buy stamps for a 60 gram letter and a packet of mass 830 grams. Copy the dial and mark on it:

    (a) the mass of the letter (use an arrow marked A);

    (b) the mass of the packet (use an arrow marked B).

    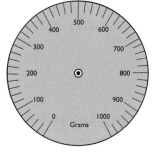

6. A vet's first two patients on Monday were a snake and a dog. He put them on the scales. The snake had a mass of $4\frac{1}{2}$ kilograms and the dog had a mass of $16\frac{3}{4}$ kilograms.

    Copy the dial and mark on it:

    (a) the snake's mass (use an arrow marked A);

    (b) the dog's mass (use an arrow marked B).

    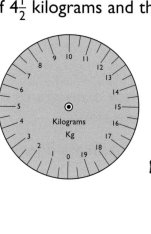

Working with mass

When we do calculations involving mass, we must think carefully about the units. For example, if we are working in grams and the answer is more than 1000, we should convert it to kilograms.

Example:

A postman has two parcels to deliver. One weighs 550 g and the other 600 g. What is the total mass of the two parcels?

550 g + 600 g = 1150 g

There are 1000 g in a kilogram, so the total mass of the parcels is 1.15 kg.

Exercise 13.2: Working with mass

1. Peter buys 250 grams of white grapes and 380 grams of black grapes. What is the total mass of grapes that Peter buys?

2. Ainsley needs 500 grams of flour to make a cake but there are only 325 grams in the flour bin. How much more flour does Ainsley need?

3. The mass of 3 members of a family is as follows: Dad is 87 kilograms, Mum 62 kilograms and Charlie is 34 kilograms. What is their total mass?

4. A chef opens a 1 kilogram bag of sugar and uses 350 grams. How much sugar is left in the bag?

5. A small jar contains 35 grams of pepper. What is the mass of pepper in 6 jars?

6. Butter is sold in packets with a mass of 250 grams. Mrs Cook needs 1 kilogram of butter. How many packets does she need?

7. A tin of beans has a mass of 450 grams.

    (a) What is the total mass of 5 tins of beans?

    (b) Is your answer more or less than 3 kilograms?

8. Clarissa makes 600 grams of peppermint creams and shares them equally between her four friends. What mass does each friend receive?

9. A recipe for 'steak supreme' requires 125 grams of steak per person. How much steak is needed for 10 people?

10. Tom, who has a mass of 90 kg, goes on a diet and loses $1\frac{1}{2}$ kg each week for 4 weeks. What is Tom's mass after 4 weeks?

Estimating mass and practical measurement

Do you know what a kilogram weight feels like? Before you start Exercise 13.3 you need to experience what a mass of 1 kg feels like. This will help you to estimate the mass of objects.

See if you can get hold of a 1 kg weight or even a bag of sugar which has mass of 1 kilogram and just feel how heavy it is. Shut your eyes and try and remember. It's a good idea if you can also handle a half kilogram (500 g) mass.

> **Tip:** When estimating a mass, it sometimes helps to hold an object whose mass you know in one hand and the object of unknown mass in the other. You can then use your hands as a balance to try and estimate the unknown mass.

Exercise 13.3: Estimating and measuring mass

1. Go around the classroom and find items that you can weigh. Give 2 answers for each item:

   (a) **Estimate** the mass

   (b) **Measure** the mass

Example:

Object	Estimate	Measurement
2 eggs	80 g	105 g
3 large potatoes	$1\frac{1}{2}$ kg	1 kg 300 g

End of chapter activity: Make a collection and investigate Imperial units of mass

1. (a) Make a collection of labels, packets, boxes, advertisements etc. that refer to mass.

   For example: You will find the mass of a packet of butter written on the wrapper. Rummage around at home and get your family to help you. (Later this could form part of a class presentation on mass.)

   (b) Record these masses and rank them in order (lightest first).

2. There is a unit of mass that is larger than a kilogram.

   (a) What is it?

   (b) What is its equivalent in kilograms?

3. Grams and kilograms are the measurements of mass we use today. They are part of what is called the **metric system**. The Imperial units were known as ounces, pounds and stones. Find out what you can about them, and make a table to show how they compare in mass with the metric units.

Did you know?

The largest known kidney stone weighed 1.36 kilograms – that's almost the same mass as one and a half bags of sugar. Imagine having that in your kidney!

The largest pumpkin weighed 377 pounds.

The largest cabbage weighed 144 pounds.

Can you work out how many bags of sugar would weigh the same as this pumpkin and cabbage?

Chapter 14: Measurement – capacity

In Chapters 12 and 13 we looked at length and mass; in this chapter we are going to look at capacity or, as it is sometimes known, volume.

Have you ever thought about how much liquid your mug holds? Have you ever measured a $\frac{1}{2}$ litre of milk to make pancake batter? In both of these examples the unit of measurement we are interested in is a **volume/ capacity** measurement.

Units of capacity

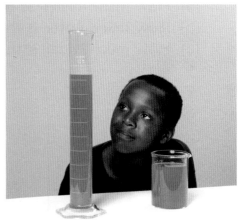

- 1000 millilitres (*ml*) = 1 litre (*l*)

- $\frac{1}{2}$ *l* = 500 *ml*

- $\frac{1}{4}$ *l* = 250 *ml*

- $\frac{3}{4}$ *l* = 750 *ml*

Reading and marking scales

Capacity scales usually go straight up. We read and mark them in the same way as the scales we met in Chapter 11.

∙ ∙

Exercise 14.1: Reading and marking scales

1.

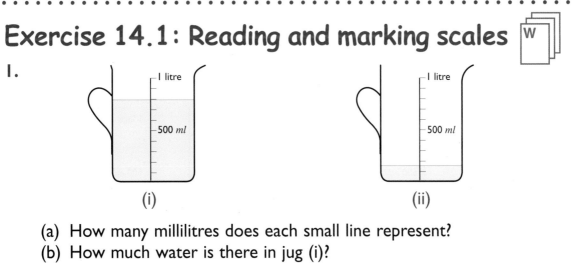

(a) How many millilitres does each small line represent?
(b) How much water is there in jug (i)?
(c) How much water is there in jug (ii)?

2.

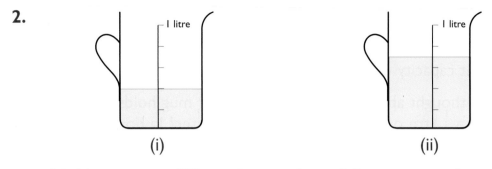

(i) (ii)

(a) How many millilitres does each small line represent?
(b) How much water is there in jug (i)?
(c) How much water is there in jug (ii)?

3.

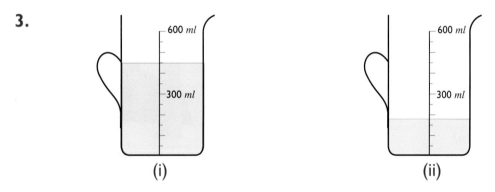

(i) (ii)

(a) How many millilitres does each small line represent?
(b) How much water is there in jug (i)?
(c) How much water is there in jug (ii)?

4. Copy the diagram below and mark:

(a) a level of 200 *ml* on jug (i);
(b) a level of 750 *ml* on jug (ii).

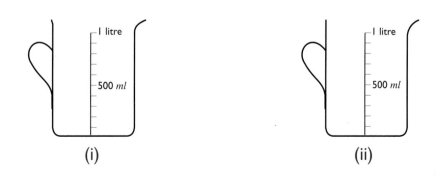

(i) (ii)

5. Copy the diagram below and mark:

    (a) a level of **800** *ml* on jug (i);
    (b) a level of **300** *ml* on jug (ii).

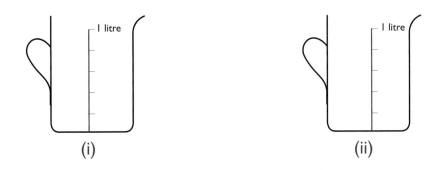

(i)   (ii)

6. Copy the diagram below and mark:

    (a) a level of **50** *ml* on jug (i);
    (b) a level of **325** *ml* on jug (ii).

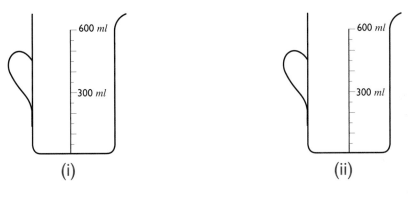

(i)   (ii)

Working with capacity

As with mass, when we do calculations involving capacity, we must think carefully about the units. For example, if we are working in litres and the answer is less than 1000, we should give the answer in millilitres. Often it is easier to convert the litres to millilitres first.

Example:

A bottle holds 2 litres of cola. Carol shares the cola equally between eight glasses. How much cola does each glass hold?

2 litres = 2000 ml

2000 ÷ 8 = 250 ml

Exercise 14.2: Working with capacity

1. A cook has two pots of cream. One contains 180 ml and the other 250 ml. She pours them both into a jug. How much cream is there in the jug?

2. The budgie's water bottle contains 60 millilitres of water. How much water is left after it drinks 18 millilitres of water?

3. A large bottle of lemonade contains 3 litres. What is the total amount of lemonade in 24 bottles?

4. An oil tank has a capacity of 500 litres. It is re-filled when there are only 75 litres left. How many litres of oil are needed to fill up the tank?

5. A medicine spoon has a capacity of 5 ml. Matron has 80 ml of cough mixture left in a bottle. How many spoonfuls of cough mixture can matron give to her patients?

6. A chef opens a new 1 litre bottle of olive oil. He uses 275 ml to make a dressing. How much oil is left in the bottle?

7. A tin bath is filled with 120 litres of water. Each day there is a loss of 3 litres due to a leak.

   (a) How much water is lost in a week?

   (b) How much water is left in the bath at the end of the first week?

8. A petrol tank is $\frac{1}{4}$ full when it has 10 litres in it. How many more litres are needed to fill the tank?

9. A bottle of lemon flavouring contains 57 ml. How much flavouring is there in 6 bottles?

10. A can of fizzy drink holds 330 ml. Mrs White wants approximately 2 litres of drink. How many cans does she need to buy?

. . . .

Estimation and practical measurement of capacity

Before you start the exercise below it is a good idea to get a litre jug and fill various different sized containers. When you fill small containers, like a thimble, you might need something like a dropper to help you. This experimenting will give you a good idea about what different capacities look like.

. . . .

Exercise 14.3: Estimating and measuring capacity

1. Get hold of several containers and find their capacity. Give 2 answers for each container:

   (a) **Estimate** the capacity

   (b) **Measure** the capacity

Example:		
Object	**Estimate**	**Capacity**
Ink bottle	75 ml	60 ml
Saucepan	3 l	2.5 l

End of chapter activity: Make a collection and investigate Imperial units of capacity

1. (a) Make a collection of labels, bottles, advertisements etc. that have capacities marked on them.

   For example: You will find the capacity of a bottle written on its label. Rummage around at home and get the family to help you. (Later this could form part of a class presentation on measurement.)

   (b) Record these capacities and rank them in order of capacity (smallest first).

2. There is a unit of capacity called a **centilitre.** Try to find out as much as possible about it.

3. Millilitres and litres are the measurements of capacity we use today. They are part of what is called the **metric system**. The Imperial units of capacity were **pints** and **gallons**. Find out what you can about them, and make a table to show how they compare in capacity with metric units.

Did you know?

The average human produces 10 000 gallons of saliva in a lifetime!

Chapter 15: Measurement revisited

Units of measurement

It is worth taking a moment to revise the units of measurement we looked at in Chapters 12, 13 and 14.

Length

The basic unit of length is the **metre**.

   10 millimetres (mm) = 1 centimetre (cm)
   100 centimetres (cm) = 1 metre (m)
   1000 metres (m) = 1 kilometre (km)

Mass

The basic unit of mass is the **gram**.

   1000 grams (g) = 1 kilogram (k)
   1000 (kg) = 1 tonne

Capacity

The basic unit of capacity is the **litre**.

1000 millilitres (*ml*) = 1 litre (*l*)

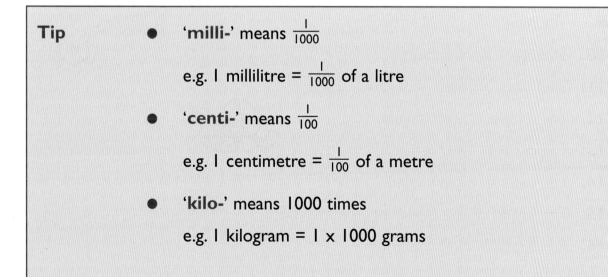

Tip	●	'milli-' means $\frac{1}{1000}$
		e.g. 1 millilitre = $\frac{1}{1000}$ of a litre
	●	'centi-' means $\frac{1}{100}$
		e.g. 1 centimetre = $\frac{1}{100}$ of a metre
	●	'kilo-' means 1000 times
		e.g. 1 kilogram = 1 x 1000 grams

Choosing units

When we measure something, we need to choose sensible units. It is much more useful to know that the distance from London to Manchester is 320 km than that it is 320 000 m. Similarly, if you measured a photo for a frame, you would say that it is 12 by 14 cm.

· ·

Exercise 15.1: Choosing units

Here are a number of units of measurement: **mm, cm, m, km, g, kg, tonne,** *ml, l.*

Write down the unit you would use to measure the following items:

1. The length of a pencil.

2. The mass of an egg.

3. The mass of a double-decker bus.

4. The capacity of a wine bottle.

5. The thickness of glass in a picture frame.

6. The distance from London to Cardiff.

7. The mass of your teacher.

8. The capacity of a small pot of cream.

9. The length of a cricket pitch.

10. The capacity of a kettle.

11. The mass of a wheelbarrow.

12. The length of a caterpillar.

13. The capacity of an egg cup.

14. The mass of a tennis ball.

15. The height of the tallest person at school.

16. The capacity of an aquarium.

17. The distance between the Earth and the Moon.

18. The mass of a full grown elephant.

19. The height of a doll.

20. The mass of a cough sweet.

. . . .

Estimation

The ability to estimate an item's length, mass or capacity is very useful. For example, you might want to work out how many bottles of lemonade you need for a party, based on your estimate of the capacity of a glass.

. . . .

Exercise 15.2: Estimation

Write down the best estimate ((a), (b), or (c)) for the size of:

1. The capacity of a glass
   (a) 2 *ml*   (b) 20 *ml*   (c) 200 *ml*

2. The height of a classroom door
   (a) 200 mm   (b) 20 cm   (c) 2 m

3. The mass of a newborn baby
   (a) 3.5 g   (b) 3.5 kg   (c) 3.5 t

4. The capacity of a teapot
   (a) 100 *ml*   (b) 1 *l*   (c) 10 *l*

5. The thickness of a sheet of cardboard
   (a) 2 mm   (b) 2 cm   (c) 2 m

6. The distance from London to Stamford
   (a) 15 000 mm   (b) 1500 m   (c) 150 km

7. The mass of a slice of bread
   (a) 5g   (b) 50 g   (c) 500 g

8. The capacity of a kitchen sink
   (a) 3000 *l*   (b) 300 *l*   (c) 30 *l*

9. The width of a piece of notepaper
    (a) 13.5 mm   (b) 13.5 cm   (c) 13.5 km

10. The mass of a lorry
    (a) 1000 g   (b) 100 kg   (c) 10 t

End of chapter activity: Presentation on measurement

Did you do the activities at the end of Chapters 12, 13 and 14? If so, now is the time to put all your efforts together and produce a really attractive and informative presentation about measurement.

Did you know?

'**Inches**', '**Feet**', **and** '**Miles**' were originally defined based on the human body.

An **inch** was the width of a thumb. A **foot** was the length of a foot. A pace was two marching steps (about 5 feet) and a **mile** was a thousand paces (5 280 feet).

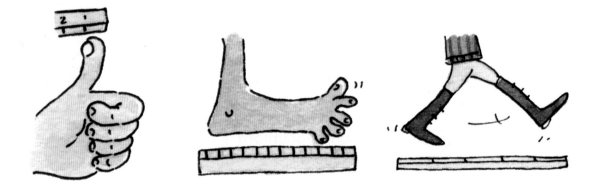

Chapter 16: Time

What do you know about time? You probably know that:

- 1 day = 24 hours

- 1 hour = 60 minutes

- 1 minute = 60 seconds

The analogue clock

You probably also know how to tell the time using an **analogue** clock.
An analogue clock has the numbers 1 to 12 marked on its face. Two hands,
one short and one long, point to the time.

Analogue clock

The analogue clock splits the day into two 12-hour halves and is often
referred to as the 12-hour clock:

- From 12 midnight to 12 midday (noon) is called **am**

- From 12 midday (noon) to 12 midnight is called **pm**

Note: **am** and **pm** come from the Latin *ante meridiem* and *post meridiem*
which mean 'before noon' and 'after noon'.

Example:

8.00 am is breakfast time.
8.00 pm is bedtime.

Exercise 16.1: Telling the time

Additional questions are available on the worksheet.

1. Write down the times shown on the clock faces below:

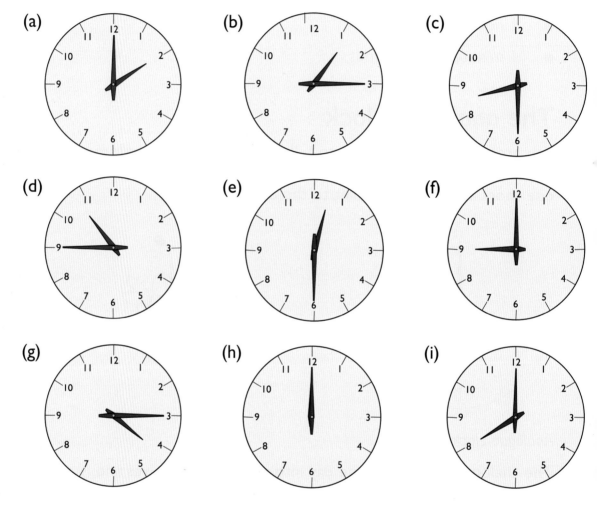

(a)   (b)   (c)

(d)   (e)   (f)

(g)   (h)   (i)

2. Write down the times shown on the following clock faces:

(a)    (b) 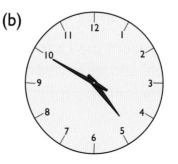   (c)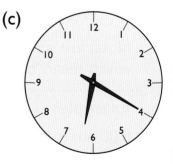

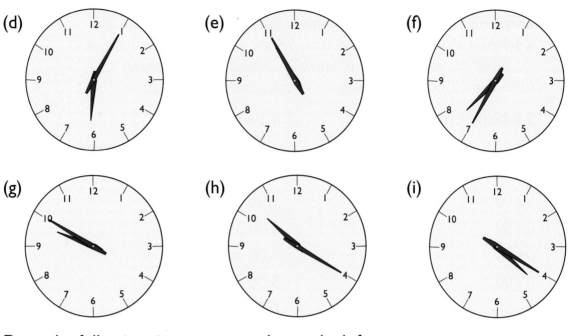

3. Draw the following times on an analogue clock face:
    (a) 2 o'clock   (b) 10 o'clock   (c) 6 o'clock
    (d) Quarter past 3   (e) Half past 11   (f) Half past 7
    (g) Quarter to 4   (h) 20 mins past 8   (i) 5 mins to 8

4. Put the following times in order giving the earliest time first:
    (a) 2 o'clock, 11 o'clock, 7 o'clock, 3 o'clock
    (b) half past 5, half past 11, half past 3, half past 2
    (c) quarter past 2, quarter past 12, quarter past 7, quarter past 10
    (d) half past 1, quarter past 1, half past 3, quarter past 7
    (e) 8 o'clock, half past 9, quarter to 8, 10 o'clock
    (f) 11 o'clock, quarter past 11, quarter past 10, quarter past 12
    (g) 4 o'clock, 15 mins past 4, 25 mins to 4, 10 mins past 9
    (h) 40 mins past 9, 20 mins past 9, half past 9

The 24-hour clock

The other common type of clock is **digital**.
A digital clock displays the time in numbers.

Digital clock showing 3 o'clock in the morning

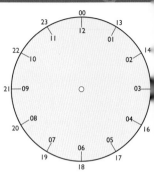

Some digital clocks show 12-hour clock times, but most are **24-hour** clocks. These use 0 to 24 for the hours, so there is no need to use am or pm. Here's a useful table to show how the 12-hour and 24-hour clock notations compare.

24-hour clock	12-hour clock
00:00	12 midnight (start of day)
01:00	1.00 am
02:00	2.00 am
03:00	3.00 am
04:00	4.00 am
05:00	5.00 am
06:00	6.00 am
07:00	7.00 am
08:00	8.00 am
09:00	9.00 am
10:00	10.00 am
11:00	11.00 am
12:00 noon/midday	12.00 noon
13:00	1.00 pm
14:00	2.00 pm
15:00	3.00 pm
16:00	4.00 pm
17:00	5.00 pm
18:00	6.00 pm
19:00	7.00 pm
20:00	8.00 pm
21:00	9.00 pm
22:00	10.00 pm
23:00	11.00 pm
24:00 midnight	12.00 midnight (end of day)

The 24-hour clock **always** uses 4 digits to give the time:

- The first 2 give the number of hours.
- The second 2 give the number of minutes past the hour.

Example:

07:45   First 2 digits for the hour (seven o'clock)

                Second 2 digits for the minutes past the hour (45 minutes past)

In the example above, the time is written with a colon. 24-hour clock times can also be written without the colon (e.g. 0745) or with a half space instead (e.g. 07 45).

Note: When using the 24-hour clock notation it is important to remember that 1 minute past midnight (24:00) is written as 00:01

Conversion from the 24-hour clock

Extension topic
As you can see from the table on the previous page, times **before 12:00** are **am** times.

Example:

06:00 is 6.00 am

11:40 is 11.40 am

Times **after 12:00** are **pm** times.

Example:

12:45 is 12.45 pm   (12:45 is a pm time but we only subtract 12 if the hour is 13 or over.)

17:20 is 5.20 pm   (17 − 12 = 5)

Exercise 16.2: Conversion from the 24-hour clock

Extension questions

Convert the following times from the 24-hour clock to the 12-hour clock. Remember to write the times using am or pm.

1. 05:00
2. 15:00
3. 22:00
4. 03:35
5. 10:10

6. 18:05
7. 23:55
8. 01:20
9. 13:55
10. 12:25

11. 14:20
12. 09:40
13. 11:50
14. 17:40
15. 21:00

16. 19:05
17. 07:10
18. 16:30
19. 20:20
20. 00:30

. . . .

Conversion to the 24-hour clock

Extension topic

Times **before noon** (am) stay the same, but remember to use **2 digits for the hour** when writing the time in 24-hour clock format.

Example:

9.20 am is 09:20

11.45 am is 11:45

For **after noon** (pm) times from 1.00 pm onwards, add 12 to the hours.

> **Example:**
>
> 12.15 pm is 12:15   (12:15 is a pm time but we don't need to change times where the hour is 12)
>
> 6.55 pm is 18:55   (6 + 12 = 18)

Exercise 16.3: Conversion to the 24-hour clock format

Extension questions
Write these times in the 24-hour clock format:

1. 6.00 am
2. 11.00 am
3. 2.00 pm
4. 7.00 pm
5. 9.15 am

6. 10.20 pm
7. 8.30 am
8. 8.30 pm
9. Midnight
10. Midday

11. 1.15 pm
12. 4.30 am
13. 6.50 pm
14. 10.45 am
15. 9.05 pm

16. 11.00 pm
17. 3.40 pm
18. 2.00 am
19. 5.00 pm
20. 5.00 am

Writing times from words

When we **write the time down** the number of minutes is always written as minutes **past** the hour. This is true for both the 12-hour and 24-hour clock.

Example:

The train leaves at a quarter past ten this evening.

This is 15 minutes **past** 10 in the evening and so is written as:

12-hour clock: 10.15 pm   or 24-hour clock: 22:15

But be careful – we do not always use minutes past the hour when we talk.

Examples:

(i)   'Your music lesson is at a **quarter to** four this afternoon.'

If you write this down, you must write the minutes as the number **past** the **previous** hour.

To find the number of minutes past the previous hour simply do the following calculation:

Number of minutes in an hour minus the stated number of minutes **to** the hour.

So in this example we calculate:

60 – 15 = 45

So we can say that 'a **quarter to** four this afternoon' is the same as 45 minutes **past** 3.

12-hour clock: 3.45 pm or 24-hour clock: 15:45

(ii)   'Breakfast will be at ten to eight tomorrow.'

Minutes must be written as minutes **past** the **previous** hour, so:

60 – 10 = 50 minutes **past** 7

12-hour clock: 7.50 am or 24-hour clock: 07:50

Tips:

- You can help yourself to become familiar with this way of thinking about time by saying, for example, 'ten forty' rather than 'twenty to eleven'.

- Here are some useful things to learn:

  Quarter past = 15 minutes past the hour

  Half past = 30 minutes past the hour

  Quarter to = 45 minutes past the hour

Exercise 16.4: Writing time from words

For the following times:

    (a) Write the time in words as minutes past the hour.

    (b) Write the time in 12-hour clock format.

    (c) Draw the time on a copy of the analogue clock face.

    (d) Write the time in 24-hour clock format on a copy of the digital clock face.

Example: A quarter to eleven in the evening becomes:

        (a) 45 minutes past 10   (b) 10:45 pm

        (c)   (d)

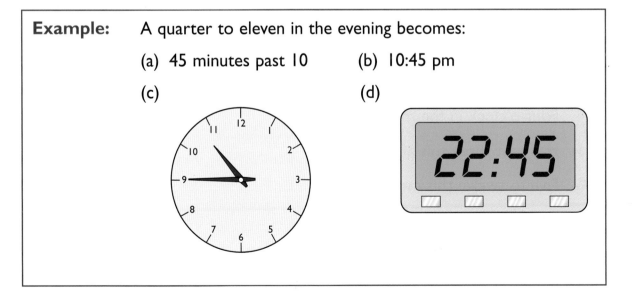

1. Half past nine in the morning.

2. A quarter to five in the afternoon.

3. A quarter past seven this evening.

4. Ten to two in the afternoon.

5. Twenty past eleven tonight.

6. Twenty to one this afternoon.

7. A quarter to midnight.

8. A quarter past midday.

9. Five minutes to ten tonight.

10. Twenty five minutes to seven this morning.

11. A quarter to eleven this morning.

12. Five past five this morning.

13. Twenty to three in the afternoon.

14. Four o'clock in the morning.

15. Half past three this afternoon.

16. Five to twelve this morning.

17. Ten to six this evening.

18. Tea and cakes will be served at four o'clock.

19. Breakfast will be at a quarter to eight.

20. Lunch is at half past one.

Conversion of hours to minutes

Now we are going to look at the connection between hours and minutes. Remember that:

$\qquad$ I hour = **60** minutes

So if we wanted to convert **hours to minutes**, we simply **multiply** the number of hours by **60**.

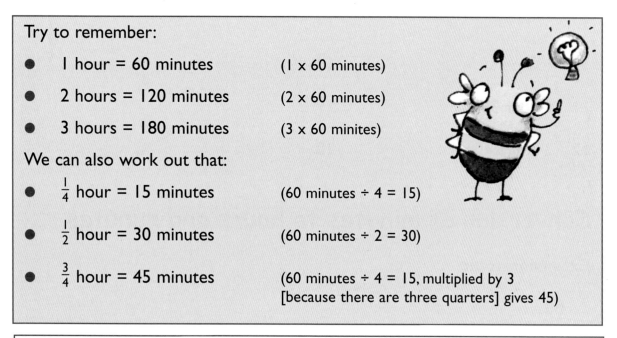

Try to remember:

- I hour = 60 minutes $\qquad$ (I x 60 minutes)
- 2 hours = 120 minutes $\qquad$ (2 x 60 minutes)
- 3 hours = 180 minutes $\qquad$ (3 x 60 minites)

We can also work out that:

- $\frac{1}{4}$ hour = 15 minutes $\qquad$ (60 minutes ÷ 4 = 15)
- $\frac{1}{2}$ hour = 30 minutes $\qquad$ (60 minutes ÷ 2 = 30)
- $\frac{3}{4}$ hour = 45 minutes $\qquad$ (60 minutes ÷ 4 = 15, multiplied by 3 [because there are three quarters] gives 45)

Example:

Convert 2 hours 25 minutes to minutes.

(2 x 60 mins) + 25 mins = 120 + 25

$\qquad\qquad\qquad\qquad$ = 145 minutes

Exercise 16.5: Conversion of hours to minutes

Give the following times in minutes:

1. I hour 10 minutes

2. 2 hours 20 minutes

3. 3 hours 40 minutes

4. I hour 30 minutes

5. 2 hours 50 minutes

6. $2\frac{1}{4}$ hours

7. $3\frac{1}{2}$ hours

8. $1\frac{3}{4}$ hours

9. 5 hours

10. 10 hours

11. 1 hour 35 minutes

12. 2 hours 40 minutes

13. $2\frac{1}{2}$ hours

14. $1\frac{1}{4}$ hours

15. 4 hours 45 minutes

16. 3 hours

17. 1 hour 55 minutes

18. $5\frac{1}{2}$ hours

19. 7 hours

20. $2\frac{3}{4}$ hours

Conversion of minutes to hours and minutes

Extension topic

Now we are going to look at things the other way round, converting minutes to hours and minutes.

To convert **minutes to hours and minutes**, we simply **divide** the number of minutes by **60**.

Example:

Convert 95 minutes to hours and minutes.

60 goes into 95 once (so 1 hour).

The remainder is 35 minutes.   (95 − 60 = 35)

So 95 minutes = 1 hour 35 minutes

Exercise 16.6: Conversion of minutes to hours and minutes

Extension questions
Convert the following number of minutes to hours and minutes.

1. 65 minutes
2. 120 minutes
3. 75 minutes
4. 180 minutes
5. 130 minutes

6. 90 minutes
7. 160 minutes
8. 240 minutes
9. 175 minutes
10. 300 minutes

11. 100 minutes
12. 135 minutes
13. 85 minutes
14. 250 minutes
15. 150 minutes

16. 80 minutes
17. 165 minutes
18. 200 minutes
19. 175 minutes
20. 105 minutes

Adding time

Once you are comfortable with what you have learnt about time so far, it is time to look at **adding minutes**.

Tip: When adding time, remember to work in **60s** (because there are 60 minutes in 1 hour).

Example:

40 minutes + 30 minutes = 70 minutes

(Ask yourself 'How many times does 60 go into 70?' The answer is once with 10 minutes remaining.)

= 1 hour 10 minutes

If you are adding hours and minutes you must do the calculation in two steps:

Step 1: First add the minutes together. If the total is more than 60 then the 'extra' hour must be carried over to the hours column (see below for how we can set this calculation out in a formal way).

Step 2: Add the hours together, plus any 'carried' hours.

Example:

2 hours 40 minutes + 1 hour 35 minutes

It is useful to set this type of calculation out in the formal way – just like we saw earlier in this book. In this case the columns are **Hours** and **Minutes**.

	Hours	Minutes
	2	40
+	1	35
	4	15
	1	

= 4 hours 15 minutes

Step 1: Add the minutes: 40 + 35 = 75 minutes, which is equivalent to 1 hour and 15 minutes (75 – 60 = 15). Carry the 1 hour to the **Hours** column.

Step 2: Now add the hours together remembering the carried hours (2 + 1 + 1).

Exercise 16.7: Adding time

Calculate:

1. 10 minutes + 50 minutes

2. 40 minutes + 30 minutes

3. 50 minutes + 35 minutes

4. $\frac{3}{4}$ hour + $\frac{1}{2}$ hour

5. 1 hour 20 minutes + 35 minutes

6. 1 hour 40 minutes + 25 minutes

7.   2 hours 25 minutes + 55 minutes

8.   2 hours 50 minutes + 1 hour 45 minutes

9.   4 hours 25 minutes + $3\frac{3}{4}$ hours

10. $2\frac{1}{2}$ hours + 1 hour 35 minutes

. . . .

Subtracting time

You also need to know how to subtract time.

As before, remember that 1 hour = **60** minutes

Example:

1 hour 10 minutes – 40 minutes

Step 1:   Convert any hours to an equivalent number of minutes.

                  1 hour 10 minutes is 60 minutes + 10 minutes = 70 minutes

Step 2:   Subtract the minutes.

                  1 hour 10 minutes – 40 minutes = 70 – 40 minutes

                                                 = 30 minutes

---

As with addition, sometimes you might want to set the calculation out in the formal way.

Example:

4 hours 25 minutes – 1 hour 40 minutes

	Hours	Minutes
	$^3\cancel{4}$	$^{60}25$
−	1	40
	2	45

Because you can't subtract 40 from 25 you have to take 60 minutes (1 hour) from the **Hours** column, to make 85 minutes (60 + 25). You can then subtract 40 from 85, to get 45

We have the answer 2 hours 45 minutes.

Exercise 16.8: Subtracting time

Calculate:

1. 1 hour − 10 minutes

2. 2 hours − 20 minutes

3. 1 hour − 25 minutes

4. 1 hour 10 minutes − 40 minutes

5. 2 hours − $\frac{3}{4}$ hour

6. 2 hours 25 minutes − 1 hour 50 minutes

7. 3 hours 30 minutes − 1 hour 50 minutes

8. 2 hours 20 minutes − $\frac{1}{2}$ hour

9. $3\frac{1}{4}$ hours − 1 hour 40 minutes

10. 5 hours − 3 hours 35 minutes

. . . .

Timetables

Timetables surround us. You almost certainly have a school timetable which tells you where to be and what you are doing on certain days and at particular times. There are also timetables for trains and buses so that people can plan what time they will leave somewhere and what time they will arrive at their destination.

Example:

Here is part of a Surrey bus timetable:

Heathside Road	1217	1247	1317
Beechwood Road	1232	1302	1332
High Street	1240	1310	1340
Odeon Cinema	1247	1317	1347

(a) Ben arrives at the bus stop on Beechwood Road at 1 pm and catches the next bus to the Odeon Cinema.

(i) Which bus does he catch?

Answer: 1302

Look along the 'Beechwood Road' row of the timetable. The first bus listed leaves at 1232, before 1 pm. The second leaves at 1302 or 2 minutes past 1. This is the bus that Ben catches.

(ii) What time does the bus arrive at the cinema?

Answer: 1317

Look at the 'Odeon Cinema' row. Make sure you write down the time in the same column as 1302

(iii) How long does the bus journey take?

Answer: 15 minutes

The hour is the same (13) in both times so you only need to look at the minutes. 17 − 2 = 15

(b) Joe lives in Heathside Road. He takes the same bus as Ben.

(i) What time does Joe get on the bus?

Answer: 1247

Look at the 'Heathside Road' row. Again, make sure you write down the time in the same column as 1302

(ii) How long does Joe's bus journey to the Odeon cinema take?

Answer: 30 minutes

This time the hours are different. You need to work out the difference between 1247 and 1317 Split the calculation into two parts:

First: work out how long it is from 1247 to 1300 There are 60 minutes in an hour. 60 − 47 = 13 minutes

Second: work out how long it is from 1300 to 1317. This is easy: 17 minutes

Third: add your two answers together. 13 + 17 = 30

Exercise 16.9: Timetables

1. Here is part of the London to Dover train timetable:

London	1510	1540	1610	1640
Chatham	1605	1635	1705	......
Sittingbourne	1610	......	1710	......
Faversham	1620	1645	1720	1750
Canterbury	1640	1710	1740	1810
Dover	1710	1735	1810	1830

(a) When does the 1610 train from London arrive in Canterbury?

(b) Which train from London arrives in Faversham at 1645?

(c) Which train from Canterbury arrives in Dover at 5.10 pm?

(d) Which station does the 1635 from Chatham not stop at?

(e) What time is the time of the last train from Sittingbourne?

(f) Which train from Chatham arrives in Dover after 1745?

(g) Trains for Dover leave London at 10 and 40 minutes past the hour. At what time will the next train leave London after 1640?

(h) Frank catches the 1510 from London. How long does he take to travel from: (i) London to Chatham; (ii) Chatham to Dover; (iii) London to Dover?

(i) How long does the 1645 from Faversham take to reach Dover?

(j) The Rev. Sexton wants to attend Evensong at Canterbury Cathedral. The Cathedral is a 5 minute walk from Canterbury station and Evensong starts at 1730. What is the time of the latest train he can catch from Chatham?

(k) Frances lives in Dover. After work she arrives at Faversham station at a quarter to six to catch a train home. How long does she wait for a train?

(l) How many minutes quicker is the 1640 train from London to Dover than the 1510 train from London to Dover?

(m) Frank returns to London on a train that leaves Dover at 1920. It takes the same time as the 1510 train from London to Dover. At what time does he arrive in London?

2. Here is an extract from Tuesday's television programme guide for Channel 99:

1600	**Teatime Tots** Stories and songs for the under fives.
1620	**Cartoon Capers** Join Mickey, Minnie, Tom and Jerry.
1700	**Cookery Class** This week: vegetables.
1745	**National News, Weather**
1830	**Local News**
1900	**School Challenge** Twitty Hall v Brains Academy
1930	**Western Street** Janice gets a surprise.
2000	**Film: The Guns Fell Silent** A saga of dash and daring. Starring Eddy Johns, Mark Jonson, Fay Steel.
2145	**Chemical Cats in Concert**

(a) How many minutes does Cartoon Capers last for?

(b) How much time is spent on news programmes?

(c) Which programmes last for three quarters of an hour each?

(d) Which programme starts at 7.00 pm?

(e) Before going out, Zac sets a 3-hour tape to record *Western Street* and the film. He adds on 10 minutes in case of problems. How many minutes of the tape will **not** be used?

3. This is part of a bus timetable:

Bus Depot	0645
Elm Street	0651
King's Avenue	0658
Grove Crescent	0703
Town Hall	0711
Railway Station	0717

Timings between the Bus Depot and the Railway Station are the same for all journeys both ways.

(a) How many minutes does it take to go from Elm Street to King's Avenue?

(b) How long does the journey take from King's Avenue to the Town Hall?

(c) Pat got on a bus which took 12 minutes to arrive at Grove Crescent. Where did Pat get on the bus?

(d) Fay's journey takes 5 minutes. Where did she get on and off the bus?

(e) At what time will the 0850 bus from the depot arrive at Grove Crescent?

(f) Mr Black catches the 0918 at King's Avenue. When does he reach the Railway Station?

(g) When does the 1004 bus from the Town Hall leave Elm Street?

(h) How many minutes does it take to go from the Bus Depot to the Railway Station?

(i) A bus leaves the Railway Station at 1128. At what time does it reach the Bus Depot?

(j) Write out in full the timetable for the journey of the 1440 bus from the Bus depot to the Railway Station.

(k) Write out in full the timetable for the journey of the 1800 bus from the Railway Station to the Bus Depot.

Problem solving

When working with time, the most important thing to remember is that there are 60 minutes in an hour. Sometimes you will need to break a calculation into more than one step, as we did when looking at timetables. You might find it helpful to make little notes as you work out your answers, so that you can keep track of what you are doing.

Exercise 16.10: Problem solving

Answer the following questions, giving your answers in the same clock format (12-hour or 24-hour) as the time in the question.

1. Sally walks to school. She leaves home at 8.15 am and arrives at 8.35 am. How long does she take to walk to school?

2. Mack starts his journey to Edinburgh at 10:00, it takes him exactly 6 hours. At what time does he arrive?

3. Fiona's music lesson lasts from 11:20 to 12:05. What is the length of the lesson?

4. Jake goes to the swimming pool to train. He practises the front crawl for 20 minutes and the breaststroke for $\frac{3}{4}$ of an hour. How long does he spend at the pool?

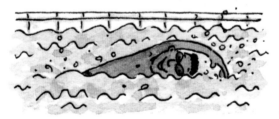

5. Steve finishes a road race in 1 hour 57 minutes, which is 4 minutes behind the winner. What is the winner's time?

6. A maths lesson, which starts at 9.45 am, is 35 minutes long. At what time does it finish?

7. Break is 40 minutes long and ends at 11:30, when does it start?

8. The football match started at 14:30 and ended at 15:40, how long was the match?

9. It takes one and three-quarter hours to cook a stew. Barbara puts it in the oven at 1.15 pm. At what time should Barbara take it out of the oven?

10. Mary gets up at 7.30 am. She spends 50 minutes dressing and having breakfast, before leaving for school. The walk to school takes her 15 minutes. At what time does she arrive at school?

11. Chicken must be cooked for 50 minutes per kilogram. How long will it take to cook a chicken with mass 3 kilograms?

12. Manuel is allowed $2\frac{1}{2}$ hours for his mathematics exam. He finishes in 1 hour 55 minutes. How much time does he have to spare?

13. Car parking charges are shown as follows:

    up to $\frac{1}{2}$ hour   **30 pence**

    up to 1 hour   **50 pence**

    1–2 hours   **£1**

    (a) Ken parks from 1420 to 1500
        How much does he pay?

    (b) Susan leaves at 0910 having paid 30 pence.
        What was the earliest she could have arrived at the car park?

14. High tide is at 1010 and the next high tide will be at 2230. How long is there between the two high tides?

15. Four children run in a relay race. They record these times:

    Peter   1 minute

    Quentin $1\frac{1}{2}$ minutes

    Robin   3 minutes

    Simon $2\frac{1}{4}$ minutes

    What is their total time in minutes?

More time equivalents

So far we have only talked about minutes and hours – there are some other periods of time that you should also be aware of. You may know some of these already:

- 1 millennium = 1000 years

- 1 century = 100 years

- 1 decade = 10 years

- 1 year = 12 months (Can you name them?)
  = 52 weeks
  = 365 days

- 1 leap year = 366 days (There is an extra day in February every fourth year.)

- 1 week = 7 days

Tip: It is very useful to know the number of days in each month. Do you? If not, here is a little rhyme which may help you to remember:

30 days hath September,
April, June and November,
All the rest have 31,
Except in February alone
Which has but 28 days clear
And 29 in each leap year.

Exercise 16.11: Summary exercise

1. Give these times in the 24-hour clock format:

(a) 9.30 am

(b) 8.45 pm

(c) 4.00 am

(d) 3.25 pm

(e) 5.05 pm

(f) 9.55 pm

(g) 10.10 am

(h) 10.10 pm

(i) 12.20 pm

(j) 12.20 am

2. Give these times in the 12-hour clock format:

   (a) 06:50   (f) 02:00

   (b) 17:10   (g) 23:50

   (c) 13:15   (h) 18:05

   (d) 20:35   (i) 11:15

   (e) 14:00   (j) 12:00

3. Write these times in the 24-hour clock format:

   (a) Twenty past six in the morning.

   (b) Five to four in the afternoon.

   (c) Ten to ten this morning.

   (d) Twenty to nine tonight.

   (e) Quarter past five this afternoon.

   (f) Five minutes to midday.

   (g) Four o'clock in the afternoon.

   (h) Half past ten tonight.

   (i) A quarter to three this afternoon.

   (j) Seven o'clock in the morning.

4. Convert the following times to minutes:

   (a) 1 hour 15 minutes   (f) $4\frac{1}{4}$ hours

   (b) 2 hours   (g) 3 hours 35 minutes

   (c) 1 hour 40 minutes   (h) 6 hours

   (d) $2\frac{1}{2}$ hours   (i) 5 hours 50 minutes

   (e) 3 hours   (j) $1\frac{3}{4}$ hours

5. Convert the following times to hours and minutes:
(extension questions):

(a) 70 minutes

(b) 90 minutes

(c) 125 minutes

(d) 85 minutes

(e) 195 minutes

(f) 240 minutes

(g) 135 minutes

(h) 200 minutes

(i) 400 minutes

(j) 165 minutes

6. (a) Add together 4 hours 35 minutes and 1 hour 45 minutes.

(b) Add together 1 hour 40 minutes and 3 hours 50 minutes.

(c) Add together $3\frac{3}{4}$ hours and 1 hour 25 minutes.

7. (a) Subtract 35 minutes from 3 hours.

(b) Subtract 2 hours 25 minutes from 5 hours 10 minutes.

(c) Subtract $1\frac{1}{4}$ hours from $1\frac{1}{2}$ hours.

8. (a) How many years are there in a century?

(b) What is the name given to a period of 10 years?

(c) How many weeks are there in a year?

(d) How many days are there in a fortnight?

(e) Which day follows Wednesday?

(f) Which month comes before September?

(g) Which month follows December?

(h) Which month has an extra day added in a leap year?

(i) How many months have 31 days?

End of chapter activity: Your school timetable

Have a look at your school timetable. Is your day well organised? Do you think you could do better? If so, what changes would you make? Imagine you are in charge and are responsible for your timetable. Make up your own timetable.

Did you know?

The names of the months in the calendar have a long history, going all the way back to the first Roman king, Romulus, in 735 BC. Romulus's calendar had only ten months:

Mars, after the Roman god of war *Mars*.

Aprilis, from the Latin *aperire*, meaning 'to open', as flowers open during this month.

Maius, after *Maia*, mother of Mercury.

Junius, after the goddess *Juno*, queen of the gods.

Quintilis, from the Latin *quintus*, meaning 'fifth'.

Sextilis, from the Latin *sextus*, meaning 'sixth'.

September, from the Latin *septem*, meaning 'seven'.

October, from the Latin *octo*, meaning 'eight'.

November, from the Latin *novem*, meaning 'nine'.

December, from the Latin *decem*, meaning 'ten'.

But having only 10 months didn't work very well so in around 700 BC two extra months were added to the calendar by King Numa:

Januarius, after the two-faced god *Janus*.

Februarius, from *Februa*, a Roman feast.

Unfortunately, this meant that the months Quintilis to December were no longer numbered correctly!

Quintilis and Sextilis were renamed July and August around 8 BC, after the emperors Julius and Augustus Caesar.

Chapter 17: Drawing and measuring lines accurately

In Chapter 12 we met the units used to measure length. In this chapter we are going to look at how we can draw accurate lines to a particular measurement. The units of length that we will use are centimetres (cm) and millimetres (mm).

10 millimetres = 1 centimetre

$5 \text{ mm} = 0.5 \text{ cm} = \frac{1}{2} \text{ cm}$

The ruler – centimetres

Have a look at your ruler. It is probably like the one pictured below.

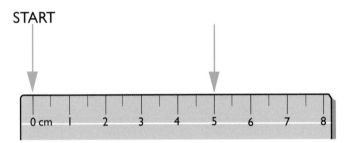

START

Whenever you measure something you must make sure you start to measure from the first mark. This first mark is shown in the diagram above. Each division represents 1 cm. In this example the distance between the arrows is 5 cm.

Lines are usually labelled with a capital letter at both ends.

When you are drawing lines, always make sure you are equipped with a sharp pencil with a hard lead and a ruler – and maybe even a rubber!

Exercise 17.1: Measuring and drawing lines (1)

1. What are the lengths of these lines?

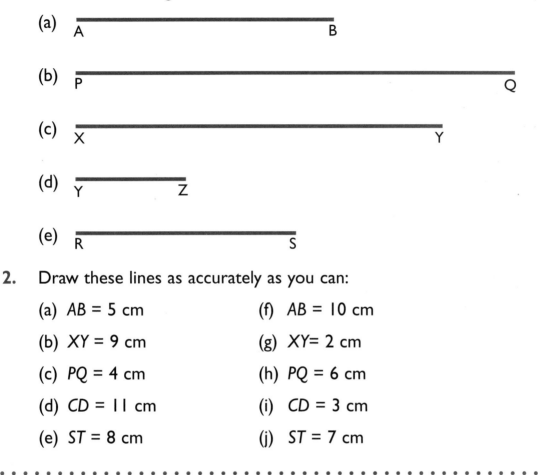

(a) A ———————————— B

(b) P ———————————————————— Q

(c) X ———————————————— Y

(d) Y ——— Z

(e) R ———————— S

2. Draw these lines as accurately as you can:

(a) AB = 5 cm   (f) AB = 10 cm

(b) XY = 9 cm   (g) XY= 2 cm

(c) PQ = 4 cm   (h) PQ = 6 cm

(d) CD = 11 cm   (i) CD = 3 cm

(e) ST = 8 cm   (j) ST = 7 cm

. . . .

The ruler – half centimetres

You may well have noticed that there are shorter lines in between the centimetre divisions on your ruler. These mark the length of half a centimetre.

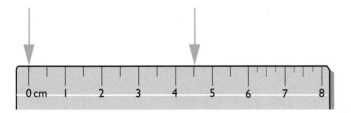

The distance between the longer centimetre mark and the shorter mark is 0.5 cm ($\frac{1}{2}$ cm).

In the diagram the distance between the arrows on the ruler is 4.5 cm ($4\frac{1}{2}$ cm).

Your ruler may even have divisions between these $\frac{1}{2}$ cm marks — these are millimetres.

Have another look at your ruler. Can you see that there are:

- $2 \times \frac{1}{2}$ cm in 1 cm;
- 5×1 mm in $\frac{1}{2}$ cm;
- 10×1 mm in 1 cm?

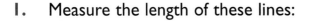

Exercise 17.2: Measuring and drawing lines (2)

1. Measure the length of these lines:

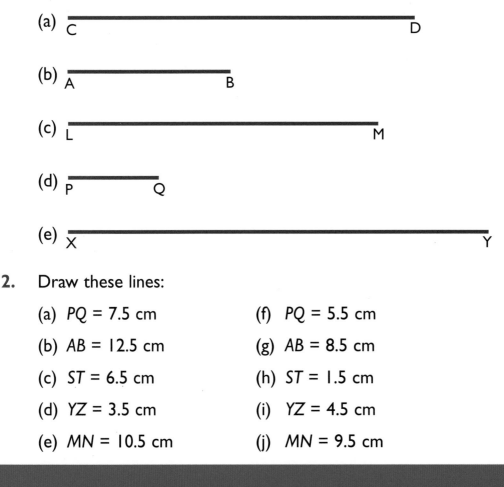

(a) C ———————————— D

(b) A ———————— B

(c) L ———————————— M

(d) P ———— Q

(e) X ———————————— Y

2. Draw these lines:

   (a) PQ = 7.5 cm   (f) PQ = 5.5 cm
   (b) AB = 12.5 cm   (g) AB = 8.5 cm
   (c) ST = 6.5 cm   (h) ST = 1.5 cm
   (d) YZ = 3.5 cm   (i) YZ = 4.5 cm
   (e) MN = 10.5 cm   (j) MN = 9.5 cm

Did you know?

The average lead pencil will draw a line 35 miles long or write approximately 50 000 English words.

Chapter 18: Position – co-ordinates

What do you do when you want to find your seat on an aeroplane? Your boarding ticket will probably give you two pieces of information, a letter and a number. You often get tickets with similar information at the theatre, cinema or football matches.

These two pieces of information help you find the **position** of your seat. In this chapter we are going to look at how this works. Here is a theatre ticket:

C 4 means that you are looking for row C and then seat number 4 in that row.

Finding and naming positions

The same idea is used to find a position on a grid of squares.

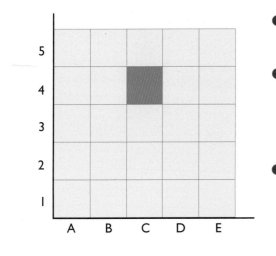

- 2 lines are drawn at right angles to each other, as shown.

- The two lines are labelled. Here, letters are placed along the bottom and numbers are placed down the left side.

- It is important to name a square correctly. The **horizontal** (along) position is given before the **vertical** (up) position; here, **letters** are written before **numbers**.

In the grid above, the shaded square is at position C4

Exercise 18.1:
Naming and finding positions on a grid

1. Name the shaded squares lettered (a) to (h).

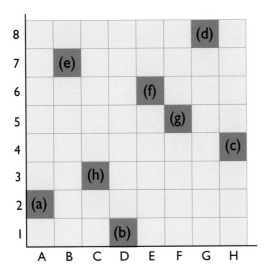

2. In this grid, the letter Q is at position E1

Write the word M A S T E R using the names of the squares.

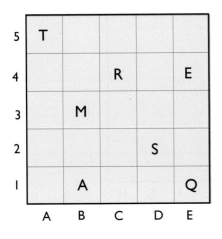

3. Look at the grid below and write 23 + 86 = 109 using the names of the squares.

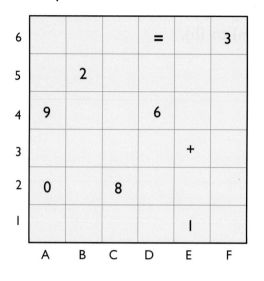

4. Copy the grid below onto squared paper, then shade and label the following squares:

(a) A is at F4

(b) B is at C6

(c) C is at B2

(d) D is at G1

(e) E is at H7

(f) F is at A5

(g) G is at D3

(h) H is at E8

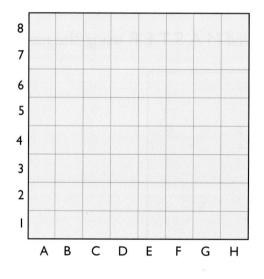

5. Copy the grid below onto squared paper, then shade the following squares:

(a) A3

(b) B3

(c) C3

(d) D3

(e) E3

(f) F1, F2, F3, F4 and F5

(g) G2, G3 and G4

(h) H3

(i) What shape is formed?

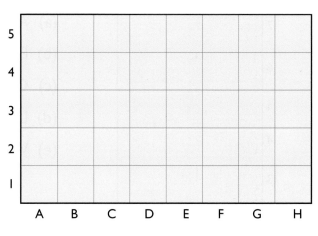

6. Copy the grid below onto squared paper, then shade the following squares:

(a) A1 and A5

(b) B1, B2 and B5

(c) C1, C3 and C5

(d) D1, D4 and D5

(e) E1 and E5

(f) What shape is formed?

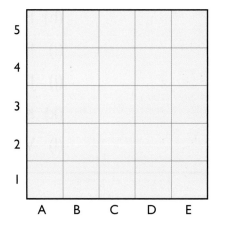

7. Copy the grid below onto squared paper, then shade the following squares:

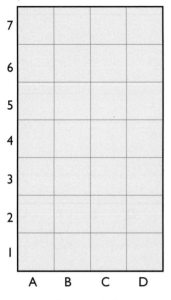

(a) A1, A2, A3, A4, A5, A6 and A7

(b) B4 and B7

(c) C4 and C7

(d) D4, D5, D6 and D7

(e) What shape is formed?

8. Copy the grid below onto squared paper, then shade the following squares:

(a) A4

(b) B3

(c) C2

(d) D1

(e) E2

(f) F3

(g) G2

(h) H1

(i) I2

(j) J3

(k) K4

(l) What shape is formed?

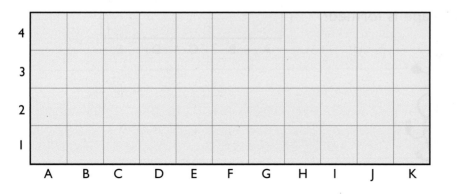

9. Copy the grid below onto squared paper, then shade the following squares:

(a) A6 and A7

(b) B1, B5, B6, B7 and B8

(c) C1, C2, C3, C4 and C5

(d) D4 and D5

(e) E4 and E5

(f) F1, F4 and F5

(g) G1, G2, G3, G4 and G5

(h) H6

(i) What shape is formed?

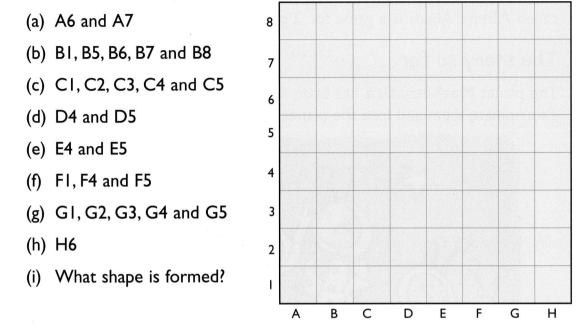

Do you think you could find your seat in a theatre now?

End of chapter activity: Aliens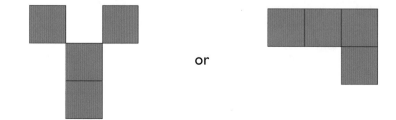

Now let's reinforce what we have learnt in this chapter by playing a game called **Aliens**. Aliens is a game for 2 people.

The story so far...

The planet **Mathematica** has been invaded by 5 aliens! Your mission is to exterminate them and free the planet from unwelcome occupation.

Preparation

First let's learn a bit more about the enemy:

● Aliens come in different shapes and sizes.

Here are two different 4-celled aliens:

or

Here are two different 3-celled aliens:

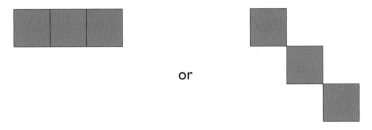

or

Here are two different 2-celled aliens:

or

There are also 1-celled aliens.

- Each player needs two 6 by 6 grids (drawn on square paper), one labelled Grid A and the other Grid B.

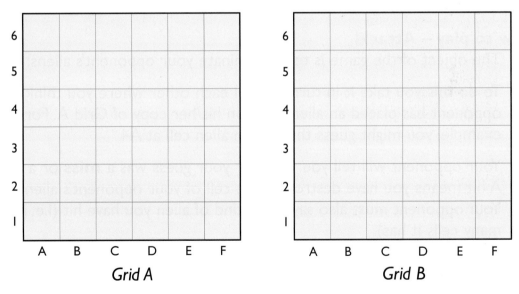

- Each player has control of:

one 4-celled alien

one 3-celled alien

one 2-celled alien

two 1-celled aliens

- Each player shades his aliens in on his Grid A (see the example below). An alien can be any shape as long as its cells are touching. Make sure each alien has the correct number of cells. Separate aliens cannot touch other.

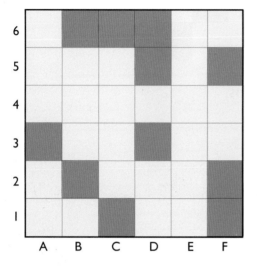

- Grid B is left untouched.

How to play – Attack!

- The object of the game is to exterminate your opponent's aliens.

- To do this you take it in turns to tell each other where you think your opponent has placed an alien's cell on his/her copy of Grid A. For example, you might guess there is an alien cell at A4

- Your opponent will tell you whether your guess was a **miss** or a **hit**. A hit means you have destroyed one cell of your opponent's alien. Your opponent must also say what kind of alien you have hit (i.e. how many cells it has).

- You then record your miss or hit result on your copy of Grid B.

- The winner is the first player to exterminate all the opponent's aliens.

Example:

Diana and Tom are playing Aliens. Diana starts the game by guessing B2. Tom says this is a miss, so Diana marks a cross at B2 on her copy of Grid B. On her second turn, Diana scores a hit on a 2-celled alien. She must then try to find the alien's second cell. Look at how she does it:

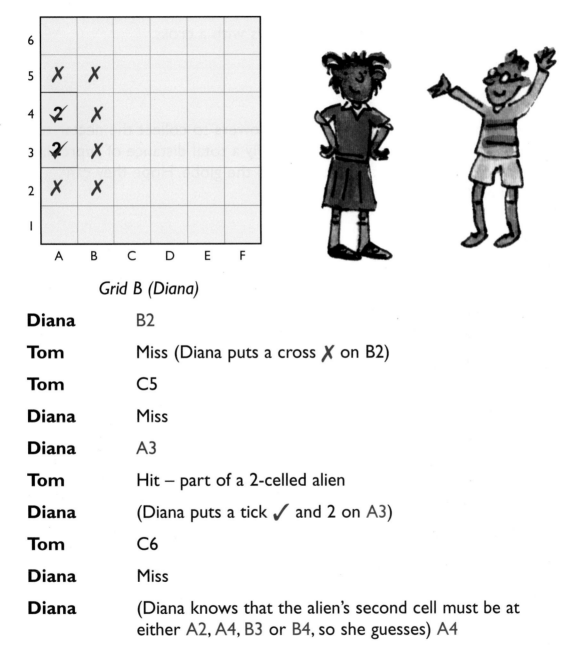

Grid B (Diana)

Diana	B2
Tom	Miss (Diana puts a cross ✗ on B2)
Tom	C5
Diana	Miss
Diana	A3
Tom	Hit – part of a 2-celled alien
Diana	(Diana puts a tick ✓ and 2 on A3)
Tom	C6
Diana	Miss
Diana	(Diana knows that the alien's second cell must be at either A2, A4, B3 or B4, so she guesses) A4

Tom	Hit – last part of 2-celled alien
Diana	(Diana puts a tick ✓ and a 2 on her A4: She has killed a 2-celled alien!)

Since separate aliens cannot touch each other, Diana now knows that there cannot be an alien cell at A2, B3, B4, B5 or A5, as well as at B2 and so she marks each of those cells with a cross.

Did you know?

A hive of bees must pollinate 2 million flowers to collect the nectar to make one pound of honey. For this they must fly a total distance of approximately 55 000 miles or more than twice around the globe. Hope they can remember where they are going!

Chapter 19: Angles and direction

One line   Two lines

When **two straight lines meet** (as in the diagram above on the right) we get an **angle**. This is sometimes referred to as the 'amount of turning' between two lines.

The **size of an angle** is measured in **degrees** (°).

Angles of 90°, 180° and 360°

We are going to investigate some very common angles. You will need a paper circle with radius 4 centimetres.

The **radius** is the distance from the centre of the circle to the middle.

A **circle** is a complete turn and measures **360°**

Follow the steps below to discover some more facts about angles and circles:

Step 1:   Fold your circle through the centre to make a semicircle: one half folds exactly onto the other half.

Step 2:   Unfold your circle and draw a line along the crease as shown below.

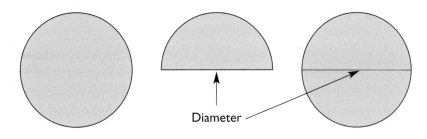

Diameter

The line you have drawn is a straight line. The angle marked around one half of this line measures 180° ($\frac{1}{2}$ of 360° = 180°)

Step 3: Take your open circle, fold it in half and in half again.

Step 4: Unfold it and draw a line along the other crease. This line will cross the first line you drew in the middle of the circle.

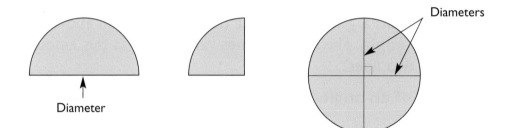

Diameters

Diameter

You have now divided your circle into four equal parts. Each angle (see one marked above) is called a right-angle.

A right-angle measures 90° ($\frac{1}{4}$ of 360° = 90° or $\frac{1}{2}$ of 180° = 90°)

Step 5: Make a list of any right angles you can see around the classroom. You can use your circle to test if an angle is more or less than 90°

Example:

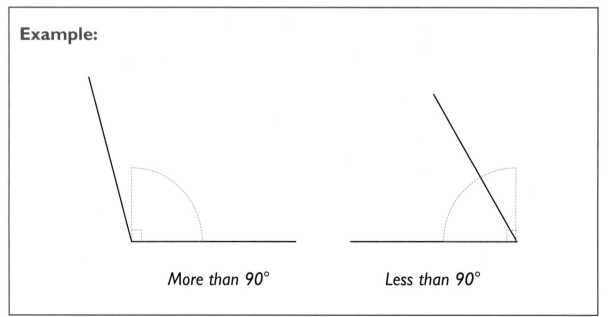

More than 90°   *Less than 90°*

Exercise 19.1:
Measuring and ordering angles

For Q1–10, use your folded circle to measure the angles. Write down whether each angle is equal to, more than or less than 90°.

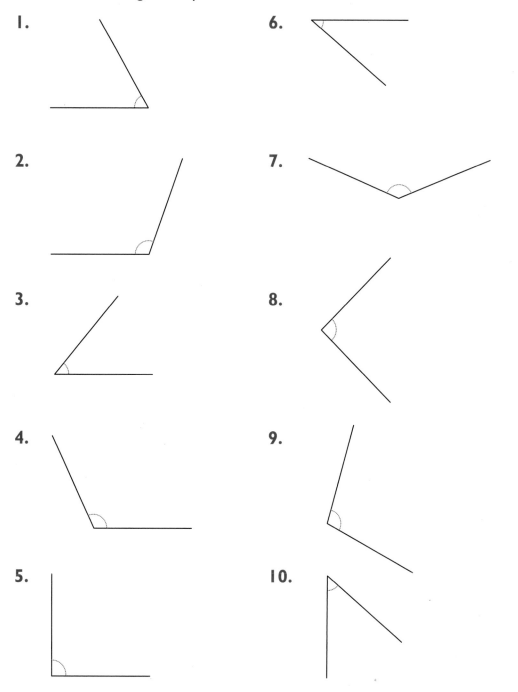

1.

2.

3.

4.

5.

6.

7.

8.

9.

10.

For Q11–18, measure the three angles using your folded circle and rank them in other of size, starting with the smallest (for example (b), (a), (c)).

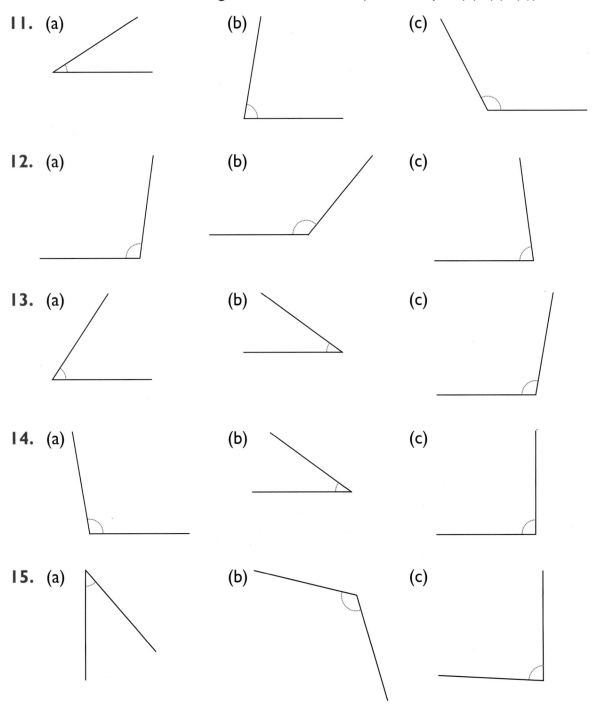

11. (a)   (b)   (c)

12. (a)   (b)   (c)

13. (a)   (b)   (c)

14. (a)   (b)   (c)

15. (a)   (b)   (c)

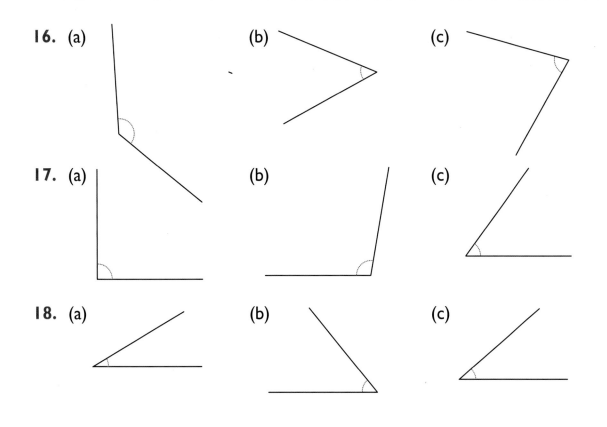

16. (a)   (b)   (c)

17. (a)   (b)   (c)

18. (a)   (b)   (c)

- -

Direction – cardinal points on a compass

The direction of something is the line or course along which an object moves. You might walk, for example, towards the white board.

To find in what direction we are walking, we can use a **compass**. A compass will tell us whether we are walking North, South, East or West. It is based on the circle you used at the beginning of this chapter. Have a look at one if you can.

There are 4 main points of the compass. These are known as the **cardinal points**. They are **North**, **East**, **South** and **West** and are spread equally clockwise around the circle with 90° (a **right-angle**) between each.

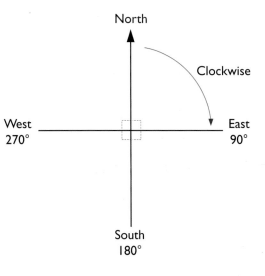

If you turned from a Northerly direction to an Easterly direction, you would turn through 90°

> **Tip:** When calculating angles between the cardinal points it is useful to know the multiples of 90:
>
> $1 \times 90 = 90$
>
> $2 \times 90 = 180$
>
> $3 \times 90 = 270$
>
> $4 \times 90 = 360$

Exercise 19.2: Points on a compass and using directions

1. Through how many degrees do you turn if you turn clockwise:

   (a) from North to East;

   (b) from North to South;

   (c) from North to West;

   (d) from East to West;

   (e) from East to South;

   (f) from East to North;

   (g) from West to East;

   (h) from South to North;

   (i) from West to South;

   (j) from South to East?

2. Look carefully at the grid below:

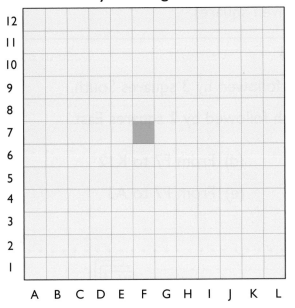

For each question below, start at the shaded square (F7) and move as instructed. Then write down the square you finish on.

Example:	2 squares East
	2 squares East from square F7 is H7

(a) 4 squares North

(b) 1 square West

(c) 5 squares East

(d) 3 squares South

(e) 2 squares North followed by 5 squares West

(f) 3 squares East followed by 4 squares South

(g) 2 squares South followed by 3 squares West

(h) 4 squares West followed by 6 squares South

(i) 3 squares North followed by 2 squares West followed by 8 squares South

(j) 4 squares East followed by 3 squares North followed by 7 squares West

3. Use the directions North, East, South and West to describe the shortest route between the given squares.

Example:	From F7 to H4
	2 squares East followed by 3 squares South.
or	3 squares South followed by 2 squares East.

(a) From F7 to A7

(b) From F7 to F1

(c) From F7 to H6

(d) From F7 to K12

(e) From F7 to A3

. . . .

End of chapter activity: A maze

1.

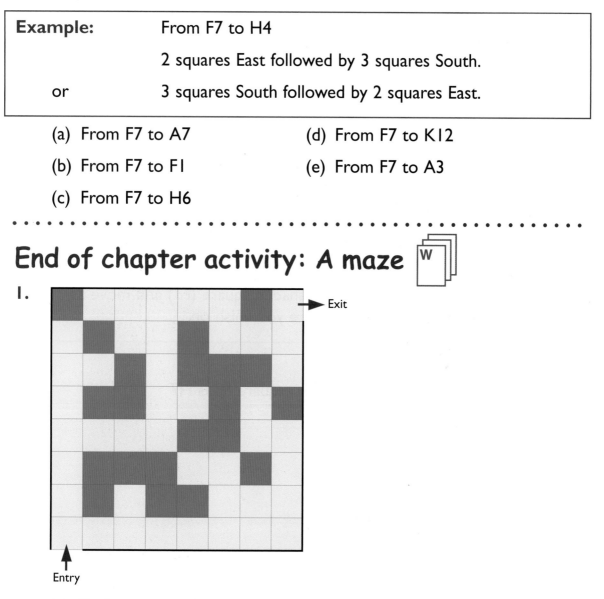

(a) Find your way through the maze.

(b) Write out your route, giving directions in terms of North, East, South and West and the number of squares you need to move. For example: North 2, West 3 and so on . . .

2. Make a maze of your own on squared paper and see whether a friend can solve it.

Did you know?

Here are two mnemonics to help you remember the order of the cardinal points on a compass, clockwise from North:

Never **E**at **S**hredded **W**heat

Naughty **E**lephants **S**quirt **W**ater

Perhaps you can invent one of your own?

Chapter 20: 2D shapes

In this chapter we are going to look at 2D shapes. You will find it useful to have a set of 2D shapes that you can handle. Your teacher will help you to gather these together:

- Circle and semi-circle

- Triangles: equilateral (three equal sides and three equal angles), isosceles (two equal sides and equal angles), scalene (no equal sides and no equal angles), right-angled, acute, obtuse

- Quadrilaterals: irregular, square, rectangle

- Polygons: irregular and regular pentagon, hexagon, octagon

All of these shapes are **flat shapes** which have **2 dimensions** (written in shorthand form as **2D**) and can be drawn on paper.

We are going to learn how to recognise 2D shapes, what they are called and what is special about them. Most of the shapes have straight sides but there are two that don't.

Circles and semi-circles

A circle   A semi-circle is half a circle

Triangles

(a)   (b)   (c)

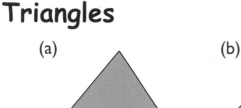
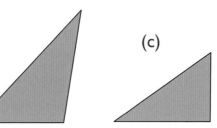

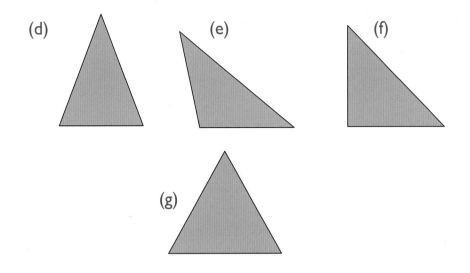

Tri- means 3

All **triangles** have **3 sides**, **3 angles** and **3 corners**. A corner is known as a **vertex**; the plural of vertex is **vertices**.

Look at the triangles above and see what you can say about the length of their sides or the size of their angles. Discuss your ideas with your teacher and your classmates.

Quadrilaterals

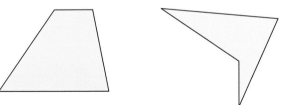

All **quadrilaterals** have **4 sides**, **4 angles** and **4 vertices**.

There are 2 special quadrilaterals which you must know:

● **Square:** All sides are equal.
               All angles are 90°

● **Rectangle**: Opposite sides are equal.
All angles are 90°

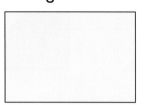

Polygons

A **polygon** means a '**many-sided figure**'. The term is usually used to describe shapes that have 5 or more sides.

A **regular polygon** has all **sides** and **angles** equal.

Here are three examples. The shapes on the left are irregular polygons. Can you see why?

● **Pentagon:** 5 sides

● **Hexagon:** 6 sides

● **Octagon:** 8 sides

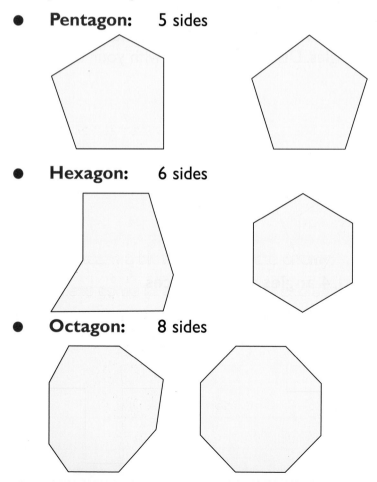

Exercise 20.1: 2D shapes

1. Name these shapes:

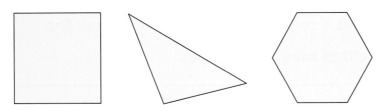

2. Draw the following shapes:

   (a) A rectangle

   (b) A circle

   (c) A pentagon

3. What name is given to all shapes that have 4 sides?

4. What name is given to the shape that has 3 angles?

5. How many vertices does an octagon have?

6. What shape is bounded by a straight line and a curve?

7. What word describes a shape that has all sides and all angles equal?

8. I have 3 sides. What am I?

9. I have 2 pairs of equal sides and all my angles are 90°. What am I?

10. I am a regular quadrilateral. What is my other name?

End of chapter activity: Make a collection of 2D shapes

1. Look around and make a collection of shapes that you can find.

2. Try constructing pictures using these shapes.

Example:

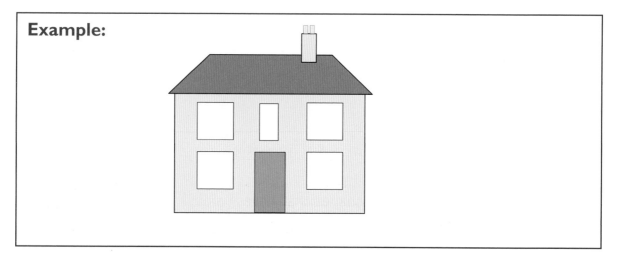

Did you know?

No piece of normal-size paper can be folded in half more than 7 times.
Try it!

Chapter 21: An introduction to line symmetry

In this chapter we are going to look at line symmetry. You will find it useful to have a set of 2D shapes that you can handle. Did you make some shapes for Chapter 20? If so, you might want to add a rhombus, parallelogram, kite, arrowhead, trapezium and isosceles trapezium.

So what is line symmetry? **Line symmetry** means that one half of a shape or pattern will map exactly on to the other half when folded. Let's find some line symmetries for ourselves!

Finding symmetry in practice

1. Draw a circle with radius 4 cm on a piece of paper, as you have done before. Cut out the circle and fold it in half. Unfold it and draw a line along the crease. This is our first **line of symmetry** – one half folds exactly onto the other.

2. Take another piece of paper and drop a blob of ink on it the centre. Then carefully fold the paper in half. Unfold it and draw a line along the crease. This is the **line of symmetry** – one half of the pattern folds onto the other.

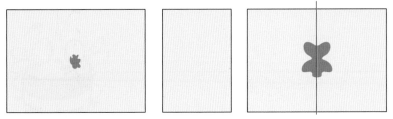

3. Take a piece of paper, fold it down the middle and make some cuts with a pair of scissors. Now unfold it and draw a line along the crease. This is the **line of symmetry** – one half of the pattern folds on to the other.

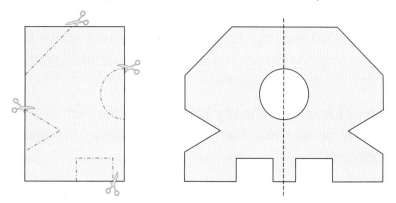

Drawing lines of symmetry

Some shapes have more than one line of symmetry.

Example:

How many lines of symmetry does a rectangle have?

A rectangle has two lines of symmetry – we can fold it along both of the lines shown in the diagram below and in each case one half exactly matches the other.

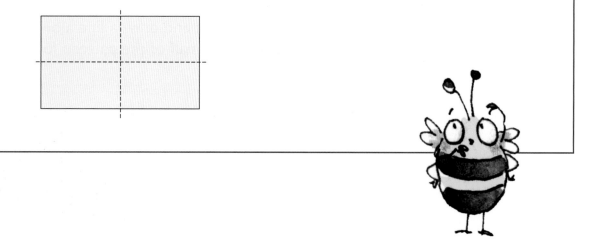

Exercise 21.1: Drawing lines of symmetry

Copy the following shapes and draw on all their lines of symmetry:

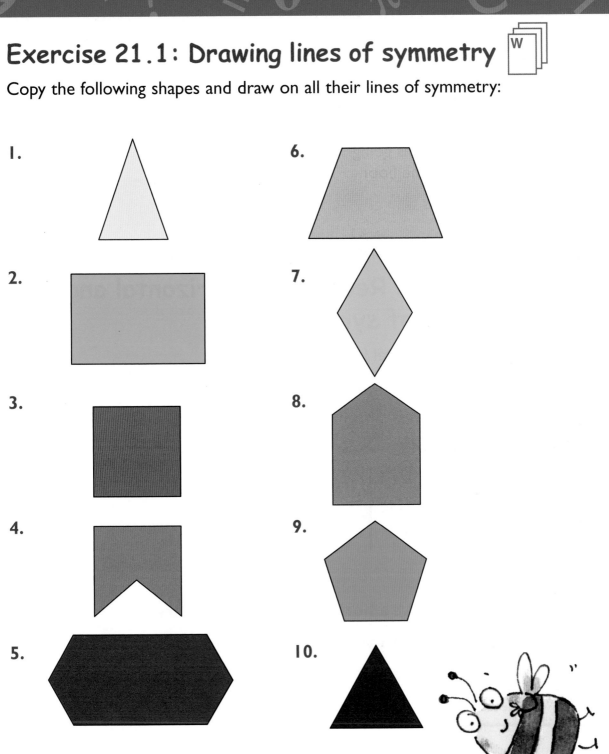

1.

2.

3.

4.

5.

6.

7.

8.

9.

10.

Recognising horizontal and vertical lines of symmetry

Here are two words it is useful to know when dealing with symmetry:

● **Horizontal** means going **across**. For example, the top of the table is **horizontal** to the floor.

● **Vertical** means **upright at 90°**. For example, the wall is **vertical** to the floor.

Exercise 21.2: Recognising horizontal and vertical lines of symmetry

Look carefully at the capital letters below.

Write down:

1. the letters that have a **horizontal** line of symmetry;

2. the letters that have a **vertical** line of symmetry;

3. the letters that have both **horizontal** and **vertical** lines of symmetry;

4. the letters that have **no** lines of symmetry.

Completing shapes with symmetry

You also need to be able to complete symmetrical shapes. Look carefully at the shape on one side of the line and make sure that what you draw on the other side matches it exactly.

Example:

In the diagram, half the shape has been drawn and the dotted line is the line of symmetry. Copy and complete the shape.

The half-shape is a triangle. Look at the point on the right. It is halfway between the other two points in a vertical direction, and one square out to the right of the line of symmetry.

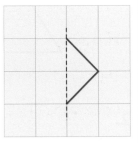

Mark another point in the equivalent place on the other side of the line, halfway between the two points in the vertical direction and one square out from the line of symmetry, this time to the left. Now join this point to the two points that lie on the vertical line of symmetry. The completed shape is a square.

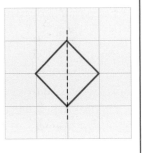

Tip: If the line of symmetry is at an angle, you might find it helpful to turn the page so that it is vertical or horizontal.

Exercise 21.3:
Completing shapes with symmetry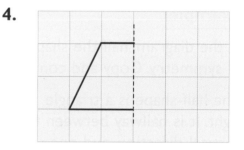

In this exercise, half the shape has been drawn and the dotted line is the line of symmetry. Copy and complete the shapes.

1.

4.

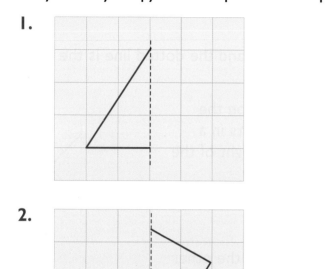

2.

5.

3.

6.

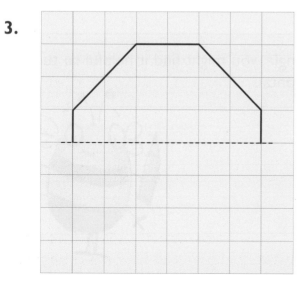

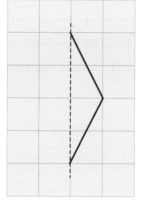

7.

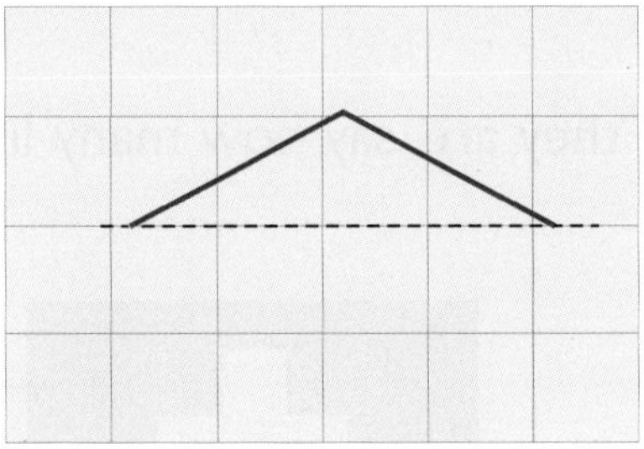

10.

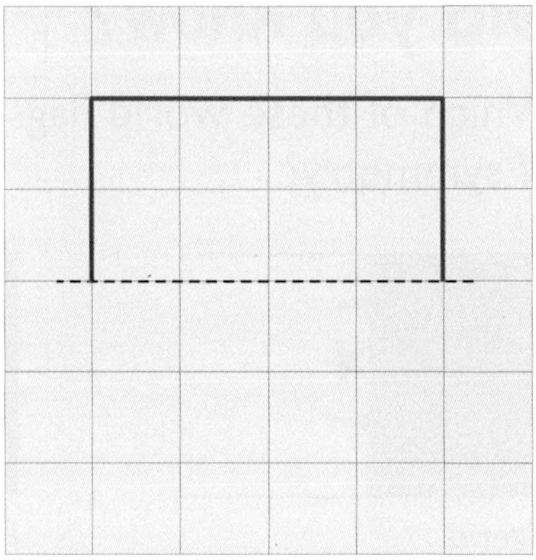

8.

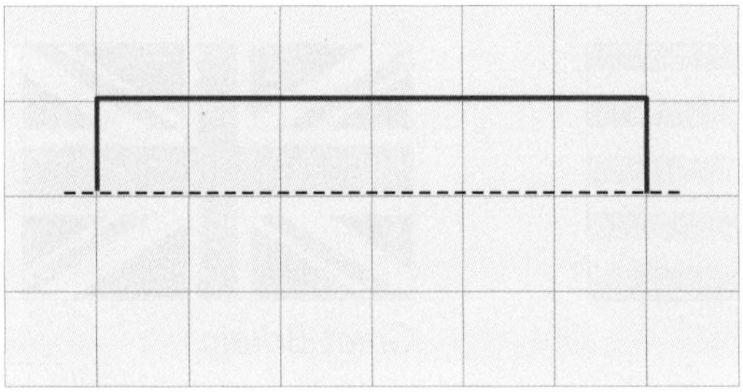

11.

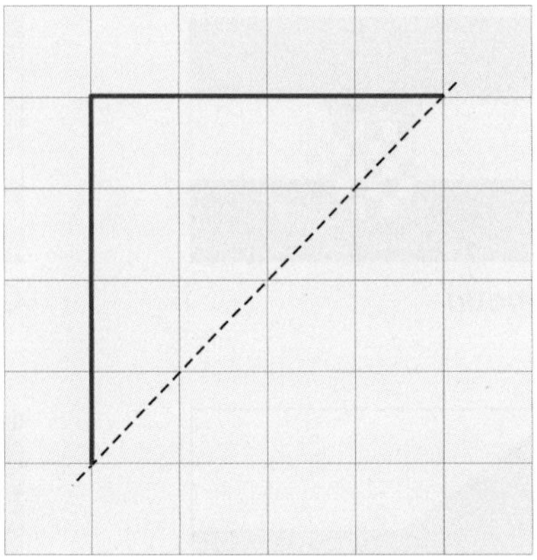

9.

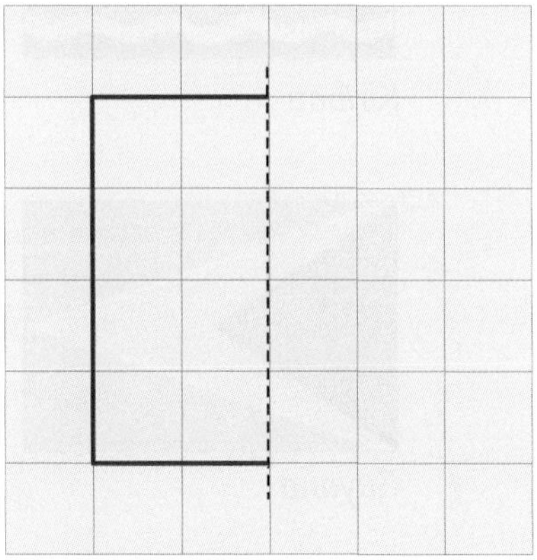

12.

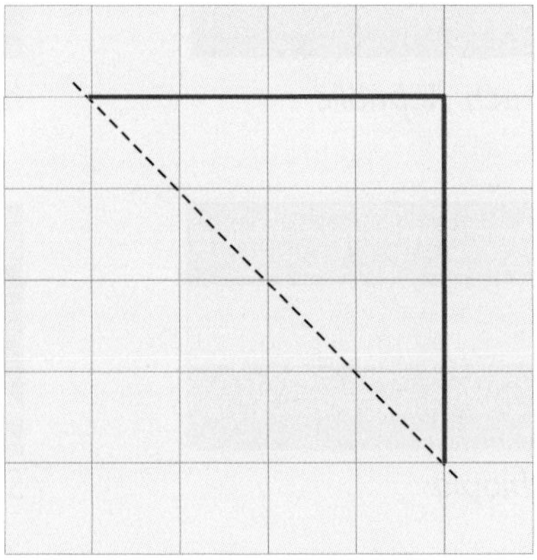

End of chapter activity: Collecting shapes with symmetry

Collect some examples of pictures that show line symmetry: magazines can be a very useful source. Sort them into sets according to how many number of lines of symmetry they have.

Did you know?

Which of these world flags are symmetrical? If they are, say how many lines of symmetry?

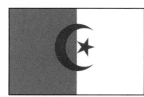

Algeria

France

Switzerland

Croatia

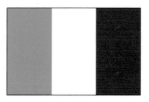

Greece

Great Britain

Czech Republic

Italy

Kiribati

Ethiopia

South Africa

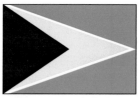

Guyana

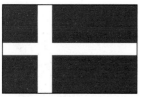

Denmark

Spain

Chapter 22: 3D shapes

In this chapter we are going to look at three-dimensional (3D), or solid, shapes. You will find it useful to have a set of 3D shapes that you can handle. Your teacher will help you to gather these together:

- Cube, cuboid, square-based pyramid, tetrahedron

- Prisms: triangular, hexagonal

Solid shapes have **3 dimensions** (written in shorthand form as **3D**). They cannot be drawn accurately on paper like 2D shapes. Don't be misled by the word **solid**, it does not mean that the shapes must be made of metal or wood; they could be filled with air!

Faces, edges and corners

Here are some useful facts about 3D shapes. Each solid figure has:

- **Faces** which are 2D shapes; faces are often flat, but not always.

- **Edges** which are straight lines where 2 faces meet.

- **Corners** (vertices) which are points where 3 or more edges meet.

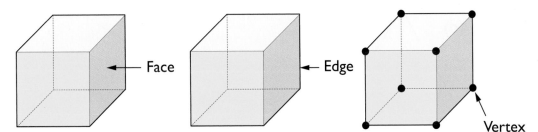

Prisms

A **prism** is a solid shape that has **the same cross-section along its length** and **2 end faces that are identical**. There are several different types of prism: two of the most common are the triangular prism and the hexagonal prism. They are named according to the shape of their end faces.

Exercise 22.1: 3D shapes

1. For each of the following shapes write down (i) the shape of the face(s), (ii) the number of faces, (iii) the number of edges, (iv) the number of vertices. Use models of the shapes to help you.

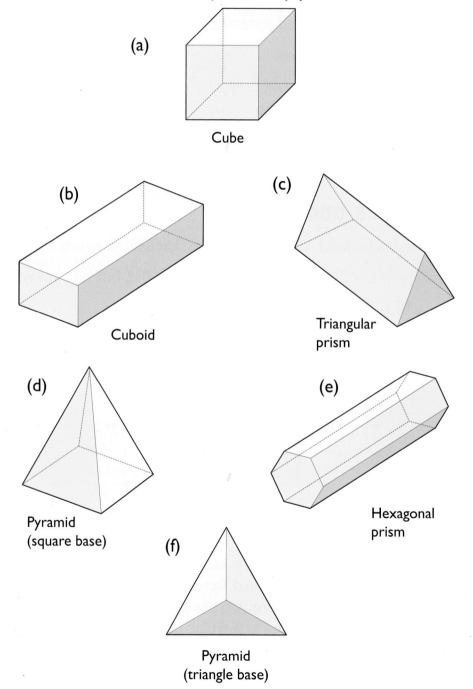

(a)

Cube

(b)

Cuboid

(c)

Triangular prism

(d)

Pyramid (square base)

(e)

Hexagonal prism

(f)

Pyramid (triangle base)

3D shapes with curved surfaces and circular faces

These solid shapes have **curved surfaces** and/or **circular faces**.

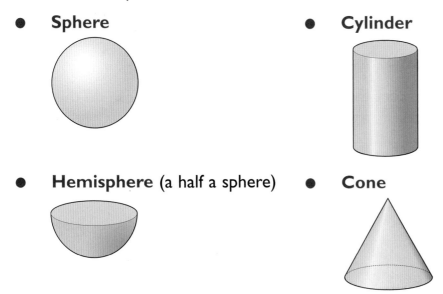

- **Sphere**

- **Cylinder**

- **Hemisphere** (a half a sphere)

- **Cone**

End of chapter activity: Make a collection of 3D shapes

Make a collection of everyday items that are examples of the solid shapes named in this chapter. Identify each one and make a display.

Did you know?

The world's largest corrugated cardboard box, was designed and manufactured by Norampac Inc. of Toronto, Canada on 15th October 2001 and measured 9.34 x 3.04 x 2.19 m (30 ft 8 in x 10 ft x 7 ft 2.5 in). Can you imagine how big this is?

Chapter 23: Carroll and Venn diagrams

Carroll and Venn diagrams are extremely useful in helping to sort information.

Carroll diagrams

Sometimes we need to sort things into groups. One way we can do this is to use a **Carroll diagram.**

Example:

Place these numbers in the correct region of the Carroll diagram: 1, 4, 8, 9, 12, 13, 15.

Even numbers	Odd numbers
4 8	1 9
12	13 15

A simple Carroll diagram

Sometimes we need to ask more than one question. Then the Carroll diagram needs more boxes divided into columns and rows. Again we decide where to put the numbers (or they could be shapes or anything else we want to sort) by asking questions. Look at the examples on the next page to see how it works.

Examples:

(i) Place these numbers in the correct region of the Carroll diagram:

3   5   6   9   10   12

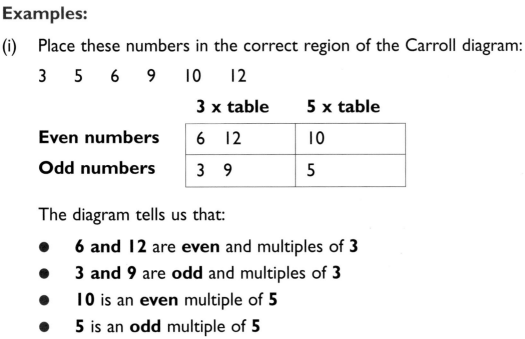

	3 x table	5 x table
Even numbers	6 12	10
Odd numbers	3 9	5

The diagram tells us that:

- **6 and 12** are **even** and multiples of **3**
- **3 and 9** are **odd** and multiples of **3**
- **10** is an **even** multiple of **5**
- **5** is an **odd** multiple of **5**

(ii) Place the following shapes in the correct region of the Carroll diagram:

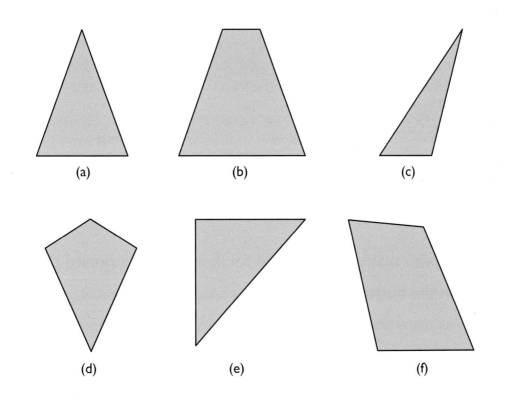

(a)

(b)

(c)

(d)

(e)

(f)

What do we know about these shapes?

- (c) is a **triangle** with **no** line of symmetry.
- (a) and (e) are **triangles** with **1** line of symmetry.
- (f) is a **quadrilateral** with **no** line of symmetry.
- (b) and (d) are **quadrilaterals** with **1** line of symmetry.

	No lines of symmetry	1 line of symmetry
Triangle	c	a e
Quadrilateral	f	b d

You can use Carroll diagrams to help you solve problems.

Example:

Sarah and Ahmed have conducted a survey. They asked all the boys and girls in their year whether they prefer English or maths. Sarah and Ahmed decide to record their results in a Carroll diagram. There are two attributes: girl/boy and English/maths.

	Maths	English
Boy		
Girl		

(a) 6 girls prefer maths. How should Sarah and Ahmed record this?

Put 6 in the bottom-left box.

(b) Twice as many boys than girls prefer maths. How many boys choose maths?

6 x 2 = 12

Put 12 in the top-left box.

(c) A quarter of the girls prefer maths. How many prefer English?

$\frac{1}{4}$ is 6 so $\frac{3}{4}$ is 6 x 3 = 18

Put 18 in the bottom-right box.

(d) The number of boys who prefer English is 4 more than the number of girls who prefer maths. How many boys prefer English?

Number of boys is 6 + 4 = 10

Put 10 in the top-right box.

(e) How many children are there in Year 5?

12 + 10 + 6 + 18 = 46

	Maths	English
Boy	(b) 12	(d) 10
Girl	(a) 6	(c) 18

Exercise 23.1: Using Carroll diagrams

1. Copy and complete the diagram for the following numbers:

9   36   4   81   64   49   25   1   100   16

	Odd numbers	Even numbers
Numbers less than 40		
Numbers more than 40		

2. Copy and complete the diagram for the following shapes (you don't need to draw the shapes – just use the letters under each shape):

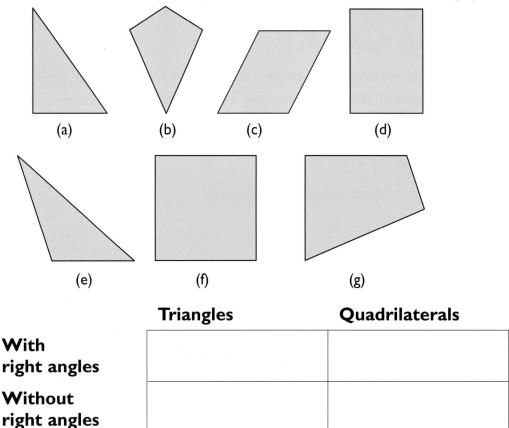

(a)   (b)   (c)   (d)

(e)   (f)   (g)

	Triangles	Quadrilaterals
With right angles		
Without right angles		

3. Tom and his sister Helen share a box of 36 dark or milk chocolates. Copy the Carroll diagram below, then use the following questions to help you complete it:

(a) How many chocolates does Tom eat?

(b) How many dark chocolates are there?

(c) How many milk chocolates does Helen eat?

	Tom	Helen
Dark chocolate	12	6
Milk chocolate	4	

4. The pupils in class J1 can choose whether to go to Gym Club or Chess Club.

    (a) Copy the Carroll diagram below, then complete it using the following information:

    ● There are 30 children in class J1.

    ● 6 boys and twice as many girls choose Gym Club.

    ● The number of girls who play chess is a quarter of the number of girls who go to the gym.

	Boys	Girls
Gym club		
Chess club		

    (b) You know the total number of children. How many boys play Chess?

5. A group of parents and children were each asked the question: 'Would you prefer to holiday in America or Europe?'

    (a) Copy the Carroll diagram below, then complete it using the following information:

    ● 12 children chose America.

    ● 8 fewer parents than children wanted to go to America.

    ● Double the number of parents wanted to go to Europe as wanted to go to America.

    ● The number of children who preferred Europe was a quarter of the total number of parents.

	Parents	Children
Europe		
America		

    (b) How many parents and children were there altogether?

Venn diagrams

A **Venn diagram** is another type of diagram that helps us to sort data and solve problems. We use circles to divide things into groups – where necessary, the groups can overlap.

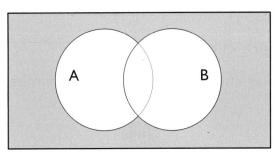

A simple Venn diagram

Note: The circles are drawn inside a rectangle – we can use the area outside the circles but inside the rectangle to record information that does not belong in either group.

A Venn diagram has two advantages:

●   It has a common area where the sets (circles) intersect.

●   It has a region within the rectangle which is outside the sets.

Examples:

(i)   Place these numbers in the correct area of the Venn diagram.

    2   4   5   7   8   10

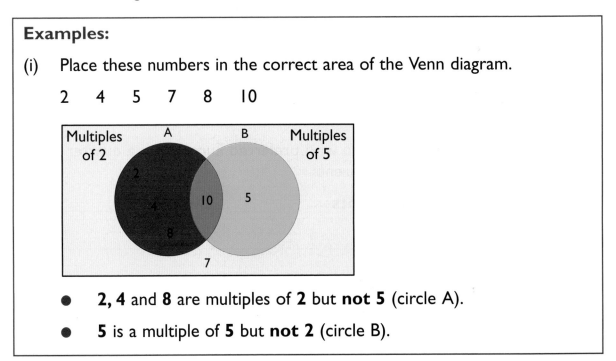

●   **2, 4** and **8** are multiples of **2** but **not 5** (circle A).

●   **5** is a multiple of **5** but **not 2** (circle B).

- **10** is a multiple of **both 2 and 5** (overlap area between the circles).
- **7** is a multiple of **neither 2 or 5** (outside the circles).

Make sure you understand why each number belongs where it does.

(ii) Place these letters in the correct region of the Venn diagram.

A BCHJTUXY

- B and C have a **horizontal** line of symmetry.
- A, T, U and Y have a **vertical** line of symmetry.
- H and X have **both horizontal** and **vertical** lines of symmetry.
- J has **neither** a **horizontal** nor a **vertical** line of symmetry.

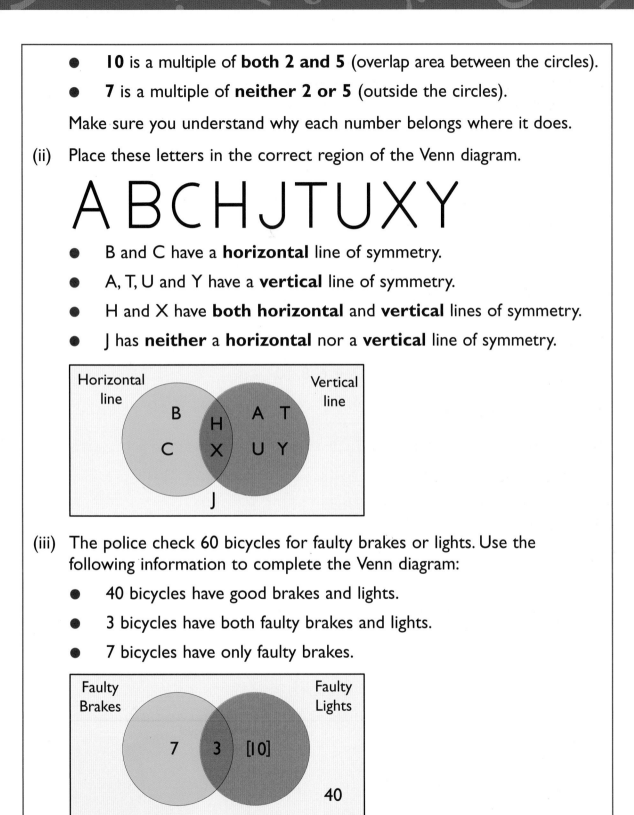

(iii) The police check 60 bicycles for faulty brakes or lights. Use the following information to complete the Venn diagram:

- 40 bicycles have good brakes and lights.
- 3 bicycles have both faulty brakes and lights.
- 7 bicycles have only faulty brakes.

To find how many bicycles had only faulty lights, subtract the number of bicycles we have been told about from the total number of bicycles checked:

Number of bicycles with only faulty lights $= 60 - (40 + 7 + 3)$

$$= 60 - 50$$

$$= 10$$

Exercise 23.2: Using Venn diagrams

1. Copy the Venn diagram below, then complete it for the numbers 1 to 10, using the following information:

   ● The numbers from 1 to 10 inclusive are 1, 2, 3, 4, 5, 6, 7, 8, 9, 10

   ● The multiples of 2 are 2, 4, 6, 8, 10

   ● The multiples of 3 are 3, 6, 9

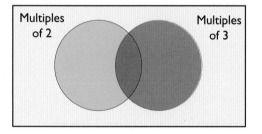

2. Copy and complete the diagram for the following shapes (you don't need to draw the shapes – just use the letters under each shape):

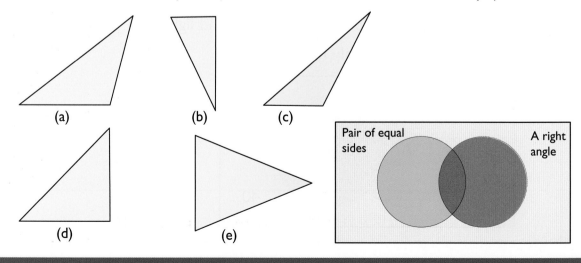

3. After their swimming lesson the pre-school group are given the choice of either an apple or a banana to eat. The Venn diagram shows their choices.

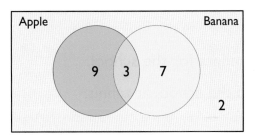

Use the diagram to answer the following questions:

(a) How many chose both an apple and a banana?

(b) How many chose only an apple?

(c) How many altogether chose a banana?

(d) How many did not choose either an apple or a banana?

(e) How many children were there altogether?

4. A group of cubs stopped for breakfast at a motorway services area.

(a) Copy the Venn diagram below, then complete it using the following information:

- 8 ate bacon and eggs.

- 4 had bacon only.

- 2 ordered only eggs.

- 3 did not have either eggs or bacon.

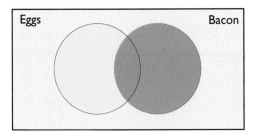

(b) How many cubs in total were there in the group?

5. St. Morag's have a rounders team and a tennis team.

    (a) Copy the Venn diagram below, then complete it using the following information:

    ● 5 girls play in both teams.

    ● 13 girls **altogether** played rounders for the school.

    ● 8 girls **altogether** represented the school at tennis.

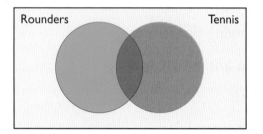

    (b) How many girls altogether played in either a rounders or tennis team, or both?

End of chapter activity: Conducting a survey and recording the results

When you plan a survey, you must think carefully about how you want to ask the questions. Some questions look as though they can be answered in only two ways – but sometimes the answer might be 'both' or 'none'.

Examples:

(i) Ask the question: 'Do you have a brother or a sister?'

    The answer could be 'brother', 'sister', 'both' or 'none'.

(ii) Ask the question: 'Do you have a dog or a cat?'

    The answer could be 'dog', 'cat', 'both' or 'none'

Ask your friends (or even your whole class or year group) the two questions in the example above and show your answers in a Venn diagram.

Did you know?

Carroll diagrams are named after **Lewis Carroll**, a famous author and mathematician. His real name was The Reverend Charles Lutwidge Dodgson (1832–1898). He was a lecturer in mathematics at Christ Church College, Oxford. As Lewis Carroll he became famous for his books *Alice's Adventures in Wonderland* and *Through the Looking Glass*.

Chapter 24: Handling data

In this chapter we are going to look at some other ways of displaying information. The charts and graphs you will meet here will be useful in everyday life as well as in other subjects, such as science.

The pictogram

Let's start by looking at a **pictogram**. As the name suggests, a **picture** or **symbol** is used to represent 1 or more 'objects'.

Example:

The pictogram below shows the number of marks achieved by 5 children in a test marked out of 10

Eve	✓ ✓ ✓ ✓ ✓	
David	✓ ✓ ✓ ✓ ✓ ✓ ✓ ✓ ✓	
Cain	✓ ✓ ✓	
Bella	✓ ✓ ✓ ✓ ✓ ✓ ✓	
Adam	✓ ✓ ✓ ✓ ✓ ✓	✓ = 1 mark

Notes:

- Always write a title at the top of your charts.

- Always work out what the symbols mean. In this case 1 tick represents 1 mark.

Have a close look at the pictogram and try and answer the following questions for yourself, before you look at the answers!

(a) Who came top?

(b) How many marks did Adam score?

(c) What was the bottom mark?

(d) What was the difference between Cain's and Eve's marks?

(e)   How many marks did Bella lose?

(f)   Which children got more than half marks?

Answers:

(a) David   (b) 6   (c) 3   (d) 2   (e) 2   (f) Adam, Bella and David

When you first see a pictogram, always start by looking at what the symbol represents.

Examples:

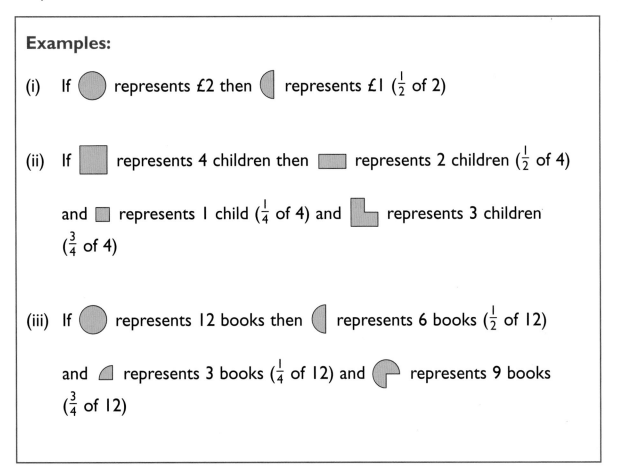

(i)   If ◯ represents £2 then ◖ represents £1 ($\frac{1}{2}$ of 2)

(ii)   If ▢ represents 4 children then ▭ represents 2 children ($\frac{1}{2}$ of 4)

and ◻ represents 1 child ($\frac{1}{4}$ of 4) and ⌐ represents 3 children ($\frac{3}{4}$ of 4)

(iii)   If ◯ represents 12 books then ◖ represents 6 books ($\frac{1}{2}$ of 12)

and ◿ represents 3 books ($\frac{1}{4}$ of 12) and ◕ represents 9 books ($\frac{3}{4}$ of 12)

Exercise 24.1: Understanding pictograms

1. The pictogram below shows the number of £1 coins saved in 6 children's piggy banks.

Keith	£ £
Joanna	£ £ £ £
Ian	
Harriet	£ £ £ £ £ £
Guy	£ £ £ £ £
Fiona	£ £ £ £ £ £ £

£ = £1

£1 coins saved in piggy bank

(a) Who has most pound coins?

(b) How many pound coins does Ian have?

(c) How many more pound coins does Guy have than Keith?

(d) How many pound coins are there altogether?

2. The pictogram below shows the number of boys and girls in the Kindergarten at Wrighton School.

Boys and girls in the Kindergarten

(a) What does 🧍 mean?

(b) How many boys are there in Reception?

(c) How many girls are there in Class 1?

(d) Which is the largest class?

(e) How many fewer girls are there in Class 2 than Reception?

(f) How many children are there in the Kindergarten?

(g) How many more boys than girls are there in the Kindergarten?

3. 5 members of the Parish Council are selling raffle tickets at the Church Fête to raise money for roof repairs. The pictogram below shows the number of tickets sold at the Church fête.

= 20 tickets

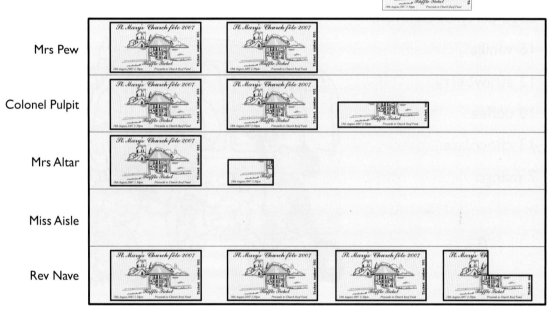

Number of tickets sold

(a) What does [image] mean?

(b) What does [image] mean?

(c) What was the most number of tickets sold by one person?

(d) Who sold the least number of tickets?

(e) How many more tickets did Colonel Pulpit sell than Mrs Pew?

(f) How many tickets were sold altogether?

(g) Tickets cost 50 pence each. How much money was raised for roof repairs?

4. Jasmin opens a packet of sweets of different colours. There are:

   8 yellow   4 green

   7 blue   2 orange

   6 pink   3 purple

   3 red   5 brown

   Draw a pictogram on squared paper to show this information. Use ◯ to represent 2 sweets.

5. Benito keeps a record of the different flavours of ice cream he sells to a large party of children:

   16 vanilla

   12 strawberry

   10 coffee

   13 chocolate

   7 mango

   Draw a pictogram on squared paper to show the information above. Use ▭ to represent 4 ice creams.

The bar chart

A **bar chart** is a **chart with rectangular bars**. These bars can be horizontal (along) or vertical (upright).

The height (or length) of the bars tells you the number of 'objects' in a group. Bar charts are very useful for comparing two or more values.

Example:

A bowl of fruit contains 12 apples, 7 bananas, 5 pears and 8 satsumas.
Show this data in a bar chart.

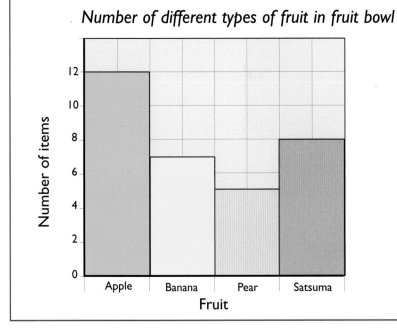

Number of different types of fruit in fruit bowl

Note:

- Always make sure your graph has a title.

- Both of the axes must have a title to explain what they represent.

- The vertical axis starts at 0 and is numbered on the lines.

- The horizontal axis tells you what the bars represent.

- The bars must always be the same width.

- You must look at the **scale** that has been used.

   In this case there are 2 pieces of fruit to each square:
   So 7 (bananas) is halfway between 6 and 8
   and 5 (pears) is halfway between 4 and 6

Exercise 24.2: Understanding bar charts

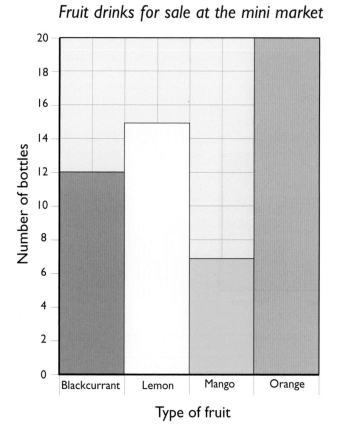

1. The bar chart below shows the number of bottles of different fruit drinks on the shelves at the mini market.

Fruit drinks for sale at the mini market

(a) How many bottles of orange are there?

(b) How many more bottles of blackcurrant are there than bottles of mango?

(c) 11 bottles of lemon are sold. How many bottles of lemon are left?

(d) Bottles of mango cost 50 pence each. All the bottles of mango are sold. How much is paid altogether for them?

2. The bar chart below shows how pupils travelled to school on Monday.

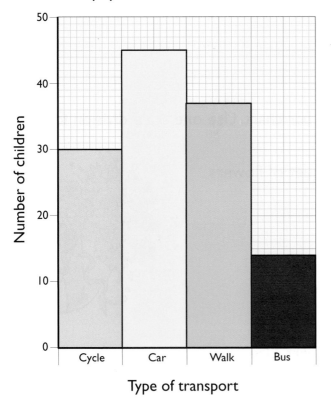

How pupils travelled to school on Monday

Think about the scale carefully before you start.

(a) How many little divisions are there for 10 children?

(b) What does 1 little division mean?

(c) What is the most common way of getting to school?

(d) How many children travelled by bus?

(e) How many more walked to school rather than cycled?

(f) 12 children were absent last Monday. How many children are there at the school?

3. The village shop stocks 4 different brands of cereal. There are:

    8 packets of Crackles

    3 packets of Scrumps

    5 packets of Honeypots

    11 packets of Sugar Crisps

    Show this information in a bar chart. Use one scale division for 1 packet on the grid.

4. Peter sends Wendy a bouquet of flowers which is made up of:

    12 carnations

    15 freesias

    7 irises

    6 roses

    Show these data in a bar chart. Use one scale division for 2 flowers on the grid.

5. The bookstall on Durlington Station sells these newspapers to the morning travellers:

    30 *Daily Mail*

    15 *Guardian*

    22 *Sun*

    47 *Daily Telegraph*

    38 *Times*

    Show these figures in a bar chart. Use a scale of 2 cm to 10 newspapers on the axis of the grid.

Frequency

The word **frequency** means **how often** something happens. In mathematics we often use **tallying** to find the frequency. 'Tallying' means counting and recording the number of times something occurs.

Each time something happens a **tally mark** is made. Tallies are grouped in fives, making it easier to check the total.

1 I   2 II   3 III   4 IIII   5 ⌿HT   6 ⌿HT I   7 ⌿HT II

Example

Count up the number of different vowels (a, e, i, o, u) in the following sentence:

Archimedes, a very famous mathematician, was born in Syracuse in Sicily.

Don't try to count all the 'a's, then all the 'e's, and so on – it is easy to make a mistake if you do it this way. Instead, look at each letter in turn: if it is not a vowel, ignore it; if it is an 'a', make a tally mark in the 'a' row of your table; if it is an 'e', make a tally mark in the 'e' row of your table; and so on.

You might use tally marks like this:

a	IIIIIIII
e	IIIII
i	IIIIIII
o	II
u	II

If you try to find the totals, you will see how difficult it is to add up the tally marks as they are written here. That is why tallying is done in 5s: 4 vertical marks and 1 diagonal.

Vowel	Tally Marks	Total
a	JHT III	8
e	JHT	5
i	JHT II	7
o	II	2
u	II	2

Now it is easy to count tallies!

Frequency graphs

Once we have recorded our information in a tally table it is useful to display it in a frequency graph. Like a pictogram or bar chart, a frequency graph represents the information as a picture, so we can tell at a glance which was the most frequent result, or which was the least frequent.

Example:

Polly shells some peas and counts how many peas there are in each pod. She records her results as follows:

5 4 6 3 2 5 6 4 6 5 7 7 5 6 6

4 6 3 6 5 5 7 6 3 2 4 6 4 3 7

4 6 7 5 3 2 3 6 5 4 5 6 4 5 4

(a) Complete the tally chart:

Peas	Tally	Frequency
2	III	3
3	JHT I	6
4	JHT III	9
5	JHT JHT	10
6	JHT JHT II	12
7	JHT	5
	Total	45

Your tallying shows how often each number of peas appears in a pod. Check your total against the original data to make sure you have not made a mistake. (There are 3 rows of 15 numbers, so 45 numbers altogether.)

(b) Show this information in a frequency graph.

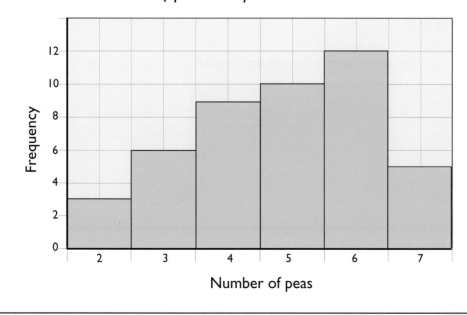

The number of peas in a pod

Exercise 24.3:
Understanding frequency graphs

1. The school football XI plays 12 matches during the term. The number of goals it scores in each match is:

2   3   1   0   2   1   3   2   4   2   0   2

(a) Copy and complete the tally chart.

Number of goals	Tally	Frequency
0		
1		
2		
3		
4		
Total		

(b) Copy the grid below and show this information in a frequency graph.

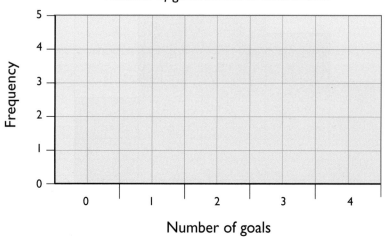

Number of goals scored in each match

2. At break, children have a choice of drinks: blackcurrant (B), lemon (L), orange (O), or water (W). A group of 42 chose as follows:

L   O   O   B   W   L   L   O   L   B   B   W   O   W

O   B   L   L   W   B   L   O   B   B   L   O   O   B

L   W   O   W   L   O   O   B   L   O   B   O   W   L

(a) Copy and complete the tally chart.

Drinks	Tally	Frequency
blackcurrant		
lemon		
orange		
water		
	Total	

(b) Copy the grid below and show the information in a frequency graph.

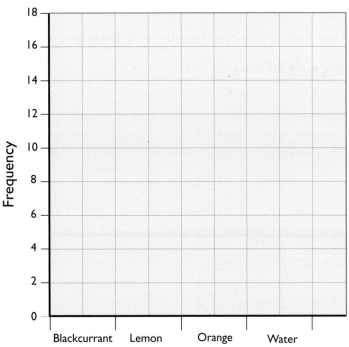

Flavours of drink chosen at break

3. Steve rolls a die 50 times and records his results:

6	2	1	3	4	3	6	5	3	1
5	1	4	1	6	2	2	4	5	2
6	2	1	3	6	4	2	5	3	4
4	1	3	2	5	6	6	2	5	3
3	5	1	6	2	5	3	2	4	6

(a) Copy and complete the tally chart.

Number on die	Tally	Frequency
1		
2		
3		
4		
5		
6		
	Total	

(b) Copy the grid below and show the results in a frequency graph.

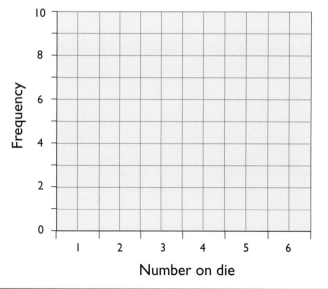

Results of rolling a die 50 times

4. Set A's mathematics exam results were:

| 52% | 63% | 65% | 46% | 68% | 67% | 71% | 64% | 69% | 70% |
| 54% | 78% | 67% | 63% | 66% | 71% | 50% | 61% | 64% | 76% |

(a) Copy and complete the tally chart.

Mark	Tally	Frequency
45%–49%		
50%–54%		
55%–59%		
60%–64%		
65%–69%		
70%–74%		
75%–79%		
Total		

(b) Copy the grid below and show the results in a frequency graph.

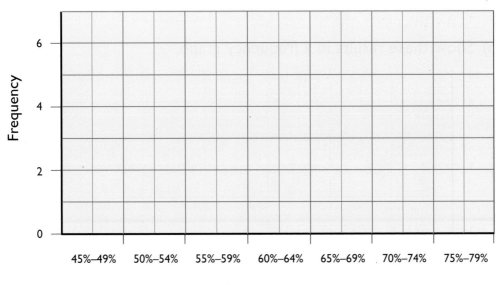

Percentage mark

5. The school doctor checked the height of 20 pupils. Here are his results measured in centimetres:

158 147 149 134 155
141 151 143 156 151
152 135 151 144 161
138 152 150 147 149

(a) Copy and complete the tally chart.

Height (cm)	Tally	Frequency
130–134		
135–139		
140–144		
145–149		
150–154		
155–160		
160–164		
Total		

(b) Show these results in a frequency graph.

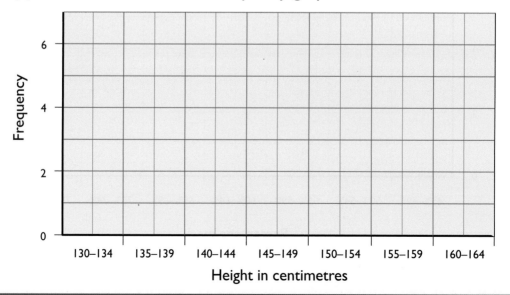

End of chapter activity: More graphs!

All sorts of information can be shown on a graph. Discuss with your teacher the possibility of drawing either personal or form graphs. You might like to investigate the size of your classmates' feet, the transport you use to get to school, favourite places for holidays, and so on. The opportunities are endless!

Did you know?

Venn diagrams are named after the **Reverend John Venn** (1834–1923) who taught at Caius College, Cambridge. There is a stained glass window in celebration of his work at Caius College: it shows one of his diagrams.

Chapter 25: Mental strategies

Teacher's introduction

The National Numeracy Strategy states that: 'In the early years children will use oral methods, in general moving from counting objects or fingers one by one to more sophisticated **mental counting strategies**. During the first few years children should be encouraged to build up a store of these strategies to enable them to manipulate and compute calculations with more ease.'

There are no right or wrong methods: not everybody will approach a mental calculation in the same way, nor need they. When a class was asked 'what is a half of 170?' the following answers were forthcoming:

Anne
$$(100 \div 2) + (70 \div 2)$$
$$= 50 + 35$$
$$= 85$$

Ben
$$(\tfrac{1}{2} \text{ of } 160) + (\tfrac{1}{2} \text{ of } 10)$$
$$= 80 + 5$$
$$= 85$$

Carol
$$(\tfrac{1}{2} \text{ of } 180) - (\tfrac{1}{2} \text{ of } 10)$$
$$= 90 - 5$$
$$= 85$$

David
$$(200 \div 2) - (\tfrac{1}{2} \text{ of } 30)$$
$$= 100 - 15$$
$$= 85$$

Eve
I just saw the answer!

None of these methods is 'better' than the others, although one wonders whether Eve is a mathematical genius or just good at guessing! What is important is not what method pupils use but whether they can explain verbally what they have done; discussion of the various methods is particularly valuable. In the end, the 'best' method is simply the one that the child is most at ease with.

This chapter does not purport to be a comprehensive catalogue of strategies; rather it sets out to suggest a few ideas that might be worth discussing.

A child should attempt a particular strategy only when the teacher thinks that child is ready to benefit from its study.

· ·

Addition

Partition

It is often possible to partition (separate) a number into tens and units. This means that the same calculation can be tackled in many different ways.

Example: 46 + 23

Think of 46 as (40 + 6) or 23 as (20 + 3)

So   46 + 23 = 46 + (20 + 3)

                    = 66 + 3

                    = 69

or   46 + 23 = (40 + 6) + 23

                    = 63 + 6

                    = 69

or   46 + 23 = (40 + 6) + (20 + 3)

                    = 60 + 6 + 3

                    = 69

Or, think of 46 as $(50 - 4)$ or 23 as $(30 - 7)$

So $\qquad 46 + 23 = 46 + (30 - 7)$

$$= 76 - 7$$

$$= 69$$

or $\qquad 46 + 23 = (50 - 4) + 23$

$$= 73 - 4$$

$$= 69$$

or $\qquad 46 + 23 = (50 - 4) + (30 - 7)$

$$= 80 - 4 - 7$$

$$= 69$$

You could in fact use the different ways of thinking of 46 and 23 in **any combination**:

$$46 = (40 + 6) \text{ or } (50 - 4)$$

and $\qquad 23 = (20 + 3) \text{ or } (30 - 7)$

Exercise 25.1: Using addition strategies

Calculate the following additions. Make sure you can explain what you did.

1. $37 + 61$
2. $45 + 34$
3. $28 + 53$
4. $19 + 39$
5. $55 + 68$

6. $96 + 52$
7. $77 + 55$
8. $96 + 68$
9. $89 + 87$
10. $74 + 95$

11. 59 + 83

12. 68 + 44

13. 72 + 98

14. 81 + 75

15. 74 + 18

16. 264 + 48

17. 128 + 81

18. 836 + 87

19. 635 + 49

20. 943 + 24

21. 265 + 187

22. 194 + 534

23. 372 + 445

24. 243 + 136

25. 346 + 234

26. 181 + 417

27. 313 + 289

28. 463 + 289

29. 364 + 236

30. 723 + 179

· ·

Use of doubles

When the numbers you are working with are close to each other, you can often use doubles.

Tip: You need to know your 2 times table for this way of thinking!

Examples:

(i) 80 + 70

Think of 80 as (70 + 10)

So $\quad\quad\quad 80 + 70 = (70 + 10) + 70$

$\quad\quad\quad\quad\quad\quad = (70 \times 2) + 10$ We have 2 lots of 70 so we put them together. We can now double 70 to give 140

$\quad\quad\quad\quad\quad\quad = 140 + 10$

$\quad\quad\quad\quad\quad\quad = 150$

Or, think of 70 as $(80 - 10)$

So $\qquad 80 + 70 = 80 + (80 - 10)$

$\qquad\qquad\qquad = (80 \times 2) - 10$ We have 2 lots of 80 so we put them together. We can now double 80 to give 160

$\qquad\qquad\qquad = 160 - 10$

$\qquad\qquad\qquad = 150$

(ii) $29 + 27$

Think of 29 as $(30 - 1)$ and 27 as $(30 - 3)$

So $\qquad 29 + 27 = (30 - 1) + (30 - 3)$

$\qquad\qquad\qquad = (30 \times 2) - 1 - 3$ We have 2 lots of 30 so we put them together. We can now double 30 to give 60

$\qquad\qquad\qquad = 60 - 1 - 3$

$\qquad\qquad\qquad = 56$

Or, think of 29 as $(28 + 1)$ and 27 as $(28 - 1)$

So $\qquad 29 + 27 = (28 + 1) + (28 - 1)$

$\qquad\qquad\qquad = (28 \times 2) + 1 - 1$ We have 2 lots of 28 so we put them together. We can now double 28 to give 56

$\qquad\qquad\qquad = 56$

Exercise 25.2: Doubling

Use doubling to calculate:

1.   50 + 60
2.   90 + 80
3.   60 + 80
4.   72 + 70
5.   63 + 60

6.   78 + 83
7.   89 + 87
8.   69 + 65
9.   24 + 29
10. 77 + 68

11. 190 + 170
12. 230 + 190
13. 195 + 190
14. 212 + 218
15. 385 + 395

16. 285 + 265
17. 465 + 455
18. 367 + 363
19. 380 + 376
20. 506 + 494

Using a number line

Another way to add two numbers is to use a number line: as you move along the line, you can make notes to help you find the answer.

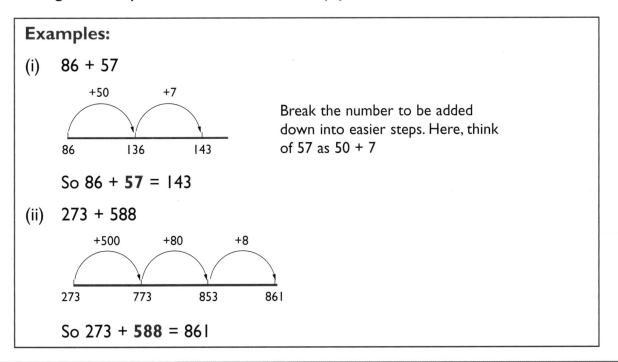

Examples:

(i)   86 + 57

So 86 + **57** = 143

Break the number to be added down into easier steps. Here, think of 57 as 50 + 7

(ii) 273 + 588

So 273 + **588** = 861

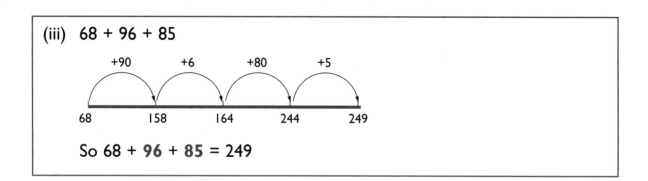

(iii) 68 + 96 + 85

So 68 + **96** + **85** = 249

Exercise 25.3: Addition using a number line

Use a number line to calculate:

1. 94 + 87
2. 47 + 58
3. 37 + 84
4. 96 + 79
5. 27 + 58

6. 17 + 66
7. 95 + 57
8. 43 + 68
9. 59 + 97
10. 89 + 74

11. 167 + 79
12. 488 + 86
13. 274 + 68
14. 376 + 54
15. 642 + 87

16. 436 + 464
17. 597 + 273
18. 746 + 168
19. 676 + 288
20. 417 + 565

21. 38 + 49 + 74
22. 63 + 91 + 55
23. 57 + 82 + 26
24. 85 + 32 + 67
25. 27 + 45 + 98

26. 475 + 39 + 86
27. 86 + 129 + 57
28. 527 + 93 + 278
29. 340 + 480 + 130
30. 186 + 234 + 405

Subtraction

Like addition, you can do subtraction in many different ways.

Counting on

When the numbers you are working with are close to each other, you can simply count on from one to the other.

Example: 93 – 88

88   89   90   91   92   93

Here you have counted on 5 to get from 88 to 93

So 93 – 88 = 5

Exercise 25.4: Subtracting by 'counting on'

Use counting on to calculate:

1. 17 – 13
2. 29 – 24
3. 38 – 31
4. 53 – 47
5. 75 – 68

6. 84 – 79
7. 72 – 67
8. 51 – 46
9. 82 – 75
10. 70 – 59

11. 112 – 107
12. 174 – 168
13. 201 – 196
14. 403 – 399
15. 506 – 498

16. 120 – 113
17. 293 – 284
18. 307 – 298
19. 517 – 509
20. 981 – 974

Counting on using a number line

If the numbers you are working with are not close together, you can count on using a number line. As before, use notes to help you find the answer.

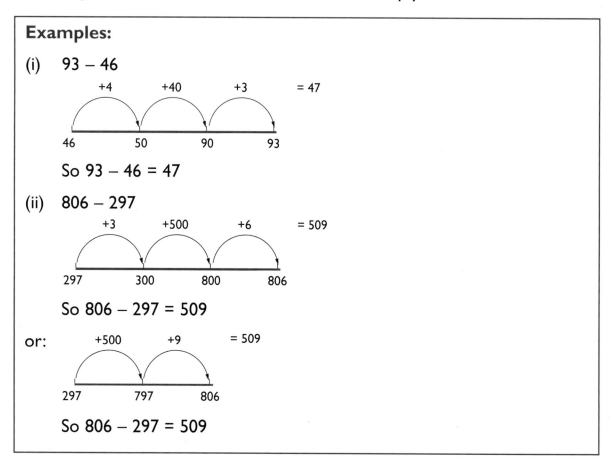

Examples:

(i) 93 – 46

So 93 – 46 = 47

(ii) 806 – 297

So 806 – 297 = 509

or:

So 806 – 297 = 509

Exercise 25.5: Subtraction with a number line (1)

Use a number line to calculate:

I. 38 – 17

2. 57 – 29

3. 82 – 38

4. 63 – 16

5. 84 – 48

6. 120 – 74

7. 131 – 87

8. 126 – 48

9. 196 – 79

10. 237 – 86

11. 275 – 196   16. 348 – 116

12. 453 – 367   17. 527 – 342

13. 821 – 713   18. 741 – 489

14. 563 – 345   19. 811 – 628

15. 742 – 578   20. 908 – 397

Counting back

When the numbers you are working with are close to each other, you might want to count back instead.

Examples:

(i)   23 – 17

23   22   21   20   19   18   17

Here you have counted back 6 to get from 23 to 17

So 23 – 17 = 6

(ii)   301 – 298

301   300   299   298

301 – 298 = 3

Exercise 25.6: Subtracting by 'counting back'

Use counting back to calculate:

1.   37 – 31   6.   87 – 79

2.   52 – 45   7.   46 – 38

3.   81 – 74   8.   57 – 46

4.   98 – 89   9.   31 – 24

5.   100 – 96   10. 17 – 8

11. 121 − 115

12. 473 − 464

13. 274 − 265

14. 315 − 308

15. 413 − 407

16. 567 − 555

17. 605 − 591

18. 777 − 768

19. 306 − 298

20. 901 − 893

Counting back using a number line

Again, if the numbers are not close together, you will find a number line useful.

Examples:

(i)   81 − 27

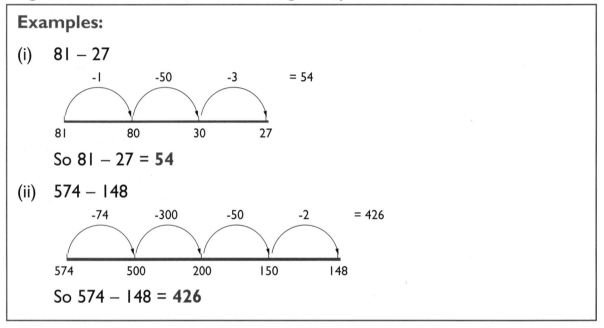

So 81 − 27 = **54**

(ii)   574 − 148

So 574 − 148 = **426**

Exercise 25.7: Subtraction with a number line (2)

Use a number line to calculate:

1.   37 − 13

2.   33 − 8

3.   42 − 27

4.   54 − 18

5.   83 − 56

6.   80 − 48

7.   64 − 39

8.   78 − 57

9.   41 − 17

10. 92 − 59

11. 240 – 176

12. 386 – 298

13. 520 – 234

14. 672 – 396

15. 816 – 429

16. 104 – 78

17. 234 – 161

18. 734 – 289

19. 969 – 572

20. 702 – 198

Addition and subtraction

Remember:

- It **does not** matter in what order you **add**:
  4 + 3 = 7 and 3 + 4 = 7

- It **does** matter in what order you **subtract**:
  9 – 5 is not the same as 5 – 9

Addition and **subtraction** are the **inverse** (opposite) of each other. If we look at the two processes together, we can see how they are connected.

Given that 65 + 17 = 82, it follows that 17 + 65 = 82

It also follows that 82 – 65 = 17

and that   82 – 17 = 65

We can use the relationship between addition and subtraction to find missing numbers.

Examples:

(i)   45 + 31 = *   * = 76   Simply add the numbers

(ii)   31 + 45 = *   * = 76   Again, add the numbers: the answer will be the same as for part (i), because the numbers are the same.

(iii) 76 – * = 45   * = 31   Subtract: 76 – 45

(iv)   76 – * = 31   * = 45   Subtract: 76 – 31

(v)   * – 31 = 45   * = 76   Add: 45 + 31

(vi)	* − 45 = 31	* = 76	Add: 31 + 45
(vii)	* + 16 = 48	* = 32	Subtract: 48 − 16
(viii)	43 + * = 80	* = 37	Subtract: 80 − 43
(ix)	* − 38 = 19	* = 57	Add: 19 + 38
(x)	45 − * = 27	* = 18	Subtract: 45 − 27

Multiplication

Let's start with some helpful hints about tables which will help us in our use of mental strategies.

The ten times and five times tables

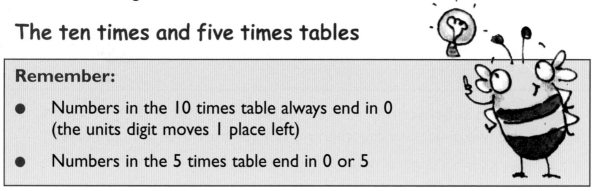

Remember:

- Numbers in the 10 times table always end in 0 (the units digit moves 1 place left)

- Numbers in the 5 times table end in 0 or 5

Since $10 = (2 \times 5)$ a multiple of 10 is twice the same multiple of 5

	10 times	5 times
(×1)	10	5
(×2)	20	10
(×3)	30	15
(×4)	40	20

To multiply by 5, multiply by 10 and **halve the answer.**

Example:	16 × 5
	$16 \times 10 = 160$ and $\frac{1}{2}$ of 160 = 80
	So 16 × 5 = 80

To multiply by 20, multiply by 10 and **double the answer.**

or   **double** and multiply by 10

Example:	12×20
	$12 \times 10 = 120$ and $2 \times 120 = 240$
	So $12 \times 20 = 240$
or	$12 \times 2 = 24$ and $24 \times 10 = 240$
	So $12 \times 20 = 240$

Note: $12 \times 10 \times 2 = 12 \times 2 \times 10 = 240$

Multiples of one hundred and multiples of fifty

Remember:

●   Multiples of 100 end in 00

●   Multiples of 50 end in 00 or 50

The two times, four times and eight times tables

Let us compare the first few multiples of each of these tables:

	2 times	4 times	8 times
(x1)	2	4	8
(x2)	4	8	16
(x3)	6	12	24
(x4)	8	16	32

$4 = 2 \times 2$ so **multiples of 4** are **twice** (double) the **multiples of 2**

$8 = 2 \times 4$ so **multiples of 8** are **twice** (double) the **multiples of 4**

or **twice** the **multiples of 2** doubled!

To multiply by 4, **double and double** again.

Example:	16 x 4
	16 x 2 = 32 and 32 x 2 = 64
	So 16 x 4 = 64

To multiply by 8, **multiply by 4** and **double the answer**

or **double** and **multiply the answer by 4**

or **double** and **double** and **double** again.

Example:	15 x 8
	15 x 4 = 60 and 60 x 2 = 120
or	15 x 2 = 30 and 30 x 4 = 120
or	15 x 2 = 30 and 30 x 2 = 60 and 60 x 2 = 120
	So 15 x 8 = 120

Note: 15 x 4 x 2 = 15 x 2 x 4 = 15 x 2 x 2 x 2 = 120

The six times table

6 = 3 x 2

To multiply by 6, **multiply by 3** and **double**

or **multiply by 2** and **treble**.

Example:	15 x 6
	15 x 3 = 45 and 45 x 2 = 90
or	15 x 2 = 30 and 30 x 3 = 90
	So 15 x 6 = 90

Note: All **multiples of even** numbers are **even**. They end in 0, 2, 4, 6 or 8

The nine times table

9 = 3 x 3

To multiply by 9, multiply by 3 and treble.

There are also some other patterns to notice.

$$1 \times 9 = 9$$
$$2 \times 9 = 18$$
$$3 \times 9 = 27$$
$$4 \times 9 = 36$$
$$5 \times 9 = 45$$
$$6 \times 9 = 54$$
$$7 \times 9 = 63$$
$$8 \times 9 = 72$$
$$9 \times 9 = 81$$
$$10 \times 9 = 90$$

Pattern 1: The **sum of the digits** of the product is **always 9 or a multiple of 9** (1 + 8 = 9, 2 + 7 = 9 and so on).

Pattern 2: The **tens digit of the product** of the first 10 multiples of 9 is **1 less than the number of nines** (1 x 9 = 09, 2 x 9 = 18, 3 x 9 = 27 and so on).

Multiplying by ten and by one hundred

When we **multiply by 10**, the digits move **1 place to the left**.

The **Units** digit moves to the **Tens** column.

Examples:

(i)   7 x 10 = 70

(ii)   15 x 10 = 150

(iii) 201 x 10 = 2010

When we **multiply by 100**, the digits move **2 places to the left**.

The **Units** digit moves to the **Hundreds** column.

Examples

(i) $4 \times 100 = 400$

(ii) $26 \times 100 = 2600$

Multiplication strategies

Partition

We can often break a multiplication down into stages by partitioning (separating) one or more of the numbers into a multiple of 10 and a unit.

Examples:

(i) $47 \times 4 = (40 + 7) \times 4$ Think of 47 as (40 + 7)

$= (40 \times 4) + (7 \times 4)$ Multiply both the 40 and the 7 by 4

$= 160 + 28$ Add the results together.

$= 188$

(ii) $78 \times 9 = (70 + 8) \times 9$

$= (70 \times 9) + (8 \times 9)$

$= 630 + 72$

$= 702$

or $78 \times 9 = 78 \times (10 - 1)$

$= (78 \times 10) - (78 \times 1)$

$= 780 - 78$

$= 702$

(iii)   83 x 13 = 83 x (10 + 3)

                = (83 x 10) + (83 x 3)

                = 830 + [(80 + 3) x 3]

                = 830 + (80 x 3) + (3 x 3)

                = 830 + 240 + 9

                = 1079

(iv)   67 x 18 = 67 x (10 + 8)

                = (67 x 10) + (67 x 8)

                = 670 + [(60 + 7) x 8]

                = 670 + (60 x 8) + (7 x 8)

                = 670 + 480 + 56

                = 1206

Exercise 25.8: Multiplication by partition

Use partition to calculate:

1. 48 x 2
2. 34 x 3
3. 27 x 4
4. 63 x 5
5. 18 x 6

6. 35 x 8
7. 23 x 7
8. 17 x 9
9. 46 x 5
10. 87 x 4

11. 18 x 16
12. 46 x 21
13. 35 x 25
14. 32 x 29
15. 54 x 18

16. 64 x 16
17. 43 x 34
18. 57 x 23
19. 38 x 31
20. 53 x 52

Use of factors

You might need to break down one or more of the numbers into its factors. Numbers that divide exactly into another number are called **factors**. For example: **3** and **6** are factors of **12**. In fact when you learn your times tables you are studying factors.

Examples:

(i)   27 x 20 = 27 x 10 x 2

                    = 270 x 2

                    = 540

     or   27 x 20 = 27 x 2 x 10

                    = 54 x 10

                    = 540

(ii)   8 x 27 = 8 x 9 x 3

                    = 72 x 3

                    = 216

Exercise 25.9: Multiplying using factors

Use factors to calculate:

1.   18 x 12   6.   26 x 16

2.   24 x 15   7.   38 x 24

3.   35 x 30   8.   56 x 40

4.   40 x 27   9.   37 x 15

5.   22 x 14   10. 63 x 32

11. 63 x 35

12. 53 x 25

13. 83 x 18

14. 67 x 24

15. 95 x 16

16. 23 x 42

17. 37 x 60

18. 72 x 48

19. 36 x 54

20. 24 x 63

Doubling

When doubling a number, look to see if you can break the calculation down by splitting the number.

Example:	Double 79
	79 x 2 = (70 + 9) x 2
	= (70 x 2) + (9 x 2)
	= 140 + 18
	= 158
or	79 x 2 = (80 − 1) x 2
	= (80 x 2) − (1 x 2)
	= 160 − 2
	= 158

Building up tables by doubling

You can build up a times table by doubling.

Examples:

(i) What is 16 x 35?

1 x 35 = 35

2 x 35 = 70   (35 x 2)

4 x 35 = 140   (70 x 2)

8 x 35 = 280   (140 x 2)

16 x 35 = 560   (280 x 2)

(ii) What is 35 x 23?

Think of 23 as 16 + 4 + 2 + 1

So 35 x 23 = (35 x 16) + (35 x 4) + (35 x 2) + (35 x 1)

$\qquad$ = 560 + 140 + 70 + 35

$\qquad$ = 805

Alternatively, think of 23 as 16 + 8 − 1

So 35 x 23 = (35 x 16) + (35 x 8) − (35 x 1)

$\qquad$ = 560 + 280 − 35

$\qquad$ = 805

Exercise 25.10: Multiplying using doubling

Use doubling to answer these questions:

1. Double 78

2. Double 69

3. (a) Copy and complete

   (i) 1 x 45 = 45

   (ii) 2 x 45 = ...

   (iii) 4 x 45 = ...

   (iv) 8 x 45 = ...

   (v) 16 x 45 = ...

   (b) Using your answers to part (a), find:

   (i) 12 x 45

   (ii) 45 x 19

4. 24 x 45

5. 32 x 45

6. 31 x 45

7. 45 x 35

. . . .

Division

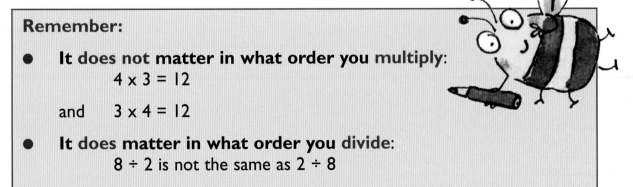

Remember:

● **It does not matter in what order you multiply:**
   4 x 3 = 12

and   3 x 4 = 12

● **It does matter in what order you divide:**
   8 ÷ 2 is not the same as 2 ÷ 8

Multiplication and **division** are the **inverse** (opposite) of each other. The connection between multiplication and division is based on tables.

Compare	A	B	C
	$1 \times 6 = 6$	$6 \div 6 = 1$	$6 \div 1 = 6$
	$2 \times 6 = 12$	$12 \div 6 = 2$	$12 \div 2 = 6$
	$3 \times 6 = 18$	$18 \div 6 = 3$	$18 \div 3 = 6$
	$4 \times 6 = 24$	$24 \div 6 = 4$	$24 \div 4 = 6$
	$5 \times 6 = 30$	$30 \div 6 = 5$	$30 \div 5 = 6$
	$6 \times 6 = 36$	$36 \div 6 = 6$	$36 \div 6 = 6$
	$7 \times 6 = 42$	$42 \div 6 = 7$	$42 \div 7 = 6$ etc

In **column A** the factors are multiplied together to give the product.

In **columns B** and **C** the product is divided by one factor; the answer is the other factor.

Given that $5 \times 6 = 30$ it follows that $6 \times 5 = 30$

It also follows that: $\quad\quad\quad\quad\quad\quad\quad 30 \div 5 = 6$

and that: $\quad\quad\quad\quad\quad\quad\quad\quad\quad 30 \div 6 = 5$

We can use the relationship between multiplication and division to find missing numbers.

Examples:

(i) $9 \times 8 = *$ $* = 72$ Multiply: 9×8

(ii) $8 \times 9 = *$ $* = 72$ Multiply: 8×9 The answer will be the same as for (i), because the numbers are the same

(iii) $* \times 9 = 72$ $* = 8$ Divide: $72 \div 9$

(iv) $* \times 8 = 72$ $* = 9$ Divide: $72 \div 8$

(v) $72 \div * = 8$ $* = 9$ Divide: $72 \div 8$

(vi) $72 \div * = 9$ $* = 8$ Divide: $72 \div 9$

(vii) $* \div 8 = 9$ $* = 72$ Multiply: 8×9

(viii) * ÷ 9 = 8	* = 72	Multiply: 9 x 8
(ix) * x 7 = 21	* = 3	Divide: 21 ÷ 7
(x) * ÷ 8 = 7	* = 56	Multiply: 8 x 7
(xi) 48 ÷ * = 6	* = 8	Divide: 48 ÷ 6
(xii) 5 x * = 45	* = 9	Divide: 45 ÷ 5

Division by ten and by one hundred

When **dividing by 10**, the figures move **1 place** to the **right**: the **Tens** digit moves to the **Units** column.

Examples:

(i)   80 ÷ 10 = 8

(ii) 500 ÷ 10 = 50

When **dividing by 100**, the figures move **2 places** to the **right**: the **Hundreds** digit moves to the **Units** column.

Examples:

(i)   300 ÷ 100 = 3

(ii) 2500 ÷ 100 = 25

Division by five

10 = 2 x 5

To **divide by 5**, **divide by 10** and **double** the answer.

Example: 80 ÷ 5

80 ÷ 10 = 8 and 8 x 2 = 16

So 80 ÷ 5 = 16

Fractions of numbers

Questions that ask you to find '$\frac{1}{2}$ of', 'a third of', 'a quarter of' and so on are really just division sums in disguise:

- 'finding $\frac{1}{2}$ of' is the same as dividing by 2

- 'finding $\frac{1}{3}$ of' is the same as dividing by 3

- 'finding $\frac{1}{4}$ of' is the same as dividing by 4

Division by two, four and eight

When dividing by two, it sometimes helps to split the number and halve each part.

Example: $76 \div 2$ Think of 76 as 70 + 6

$\frac{1}{2}$ of 70 = **35**

$\frac{1}{2}$ of 6 = **3**

So $76 \div 2 = (35 + 3) = 38$

$4 = 2 \times 2$ and $\frac{1}{4} = \frac{1}{2}$ of a $\frac{1}{2}$

To **divide by 4**, **divide by 2** and **divide by 2 again**.

Example: $68 \div 4$

$68 \div 2 = 34$ and $34 \div 2 = 17$

So $68 \div 4 = 17$

$8 = 2 \times 2 \times 2$ and $\frac{1}{8} = \frac{1}{2}$ of a $\frac{1}{4}$ or $\frac{1}{2}$ of a $\frac{1}{2}$ of a $\frac{1}{2}$

To **divide by 8, divide by 2, divide by 2** and **divide by 2 again!**

Example: $96 \div 8$

$96 \div 2 = 48$ and $48 \div 2 = 24$ and $24 \div 2 = 12$

So $96 \div 8 = 12$

Division using multiples of 10

You can think of division as repeated subtraction. Start by subtracting multiples of 10

Example: $84 \div 3$

$$84$$

$- \ 30$ (10 lots of 3)

$$54$$

$- \ 30$ (10 lots of 3)

$$24$$

$- \ 24$ (8 lots of 3)

$$00$$

So $84 \div 3 = 28$ $(10 + 10 + 8)$

Exercise 25.11: Division

Calculate the following using methods we have seen above:

1. $70 \div 10$
2. $450 \div 10$
3. $600 \div 100$
4. $7000 \div 100$
5. $60 \div 5$

6. $110 \div 5$
7. $240 \div 5$
8. $90 \div 2$
9. $78 \div 2$
10. $100 \div 4$

11. $76 \div 4$
12. $132 \div 4$
13. $200 \div 8$
14. $128 \div 8$
15. $416 \div 8$

16. $\frac{1}{2}$ of 94
17. $\frac{1}{4}$ of 120
18. $\frac{1}{8}$ of 400
19. $\frac{1}{5}$ of 230
20. $\frac{1}{10}$ of 160

21. $57 \div 3$
22. $84 \div 6$
23. $105 \div 7$
24. $126 \div 9$
25. $85 \div 5$

26. $162 \div 3$
27. $192 \div 6$
28. $259 \div 7$
29. $285 \div 5$
30. $387 \div 9$

Now that you have come to the end of the book you should have a very good feel for the way numbers behave and know how exciting it can be when you discover yet another way of playing around with them.

Did you know?

Here is a bit of fun before you go!

While sitting at your desk make clockwise circles with your right foot. Go ahead no one will see you! While doing this, draw the number '6' in the air with your right hand. Can you do it?

I look forward to meeting you again in Junior Maths Book 2!

Index